The Elements of Moral Philosophy

NINTH EDITION

JAMES RACHELS

Editions 5-9 by

STUART RACHELS

Mc
Graw
Hill
Education

THE ELEMENTS OF MORAL PHILOSOPHY, NINTH EDITION

Published by McGraw-Hill Education, 2 Penn Plaza, New York, NY 10121. Copyright © 2019 by McGraw-Hill Education. All rights reserved. Printed in the United States of America. Previous editions © 2015, 2012, and 2010. No part of this publication may be reproduced or distributed in any form or by any means, or stored in a database or retrieval system, without the prior written consent of McGraw-Hill Education, including, but not limited to, in any network or other electronic storage or transmission, or broadcast for distance learning.

Some ancillaries, including electronic and print components, may not be available to customers outside the United States.

This book is printed on acid-free paper.

1 2 3 4 5 6 7 8 9 LCR 21 20 19 18

ISBN 978-1-259-91425-6
MHID 1-259-91425-9

Portfolio Manager: *Jamie Laferrera*
Product Developer: *Erika Lo*
Marketing Manager: *Nancy Baudean*
Content Project Manager: *Maria McGreal*
Buyer: *Susan K. Culbertson*
Design: *Lumina Datamatics, Inc.*
Content Licensing Specialist: *Melisa Seegmiller*
Cover Image: *©T.A.Rector (NRAO/AUI/NSF and NOAO/AURA/NSF) and B.A.Wolpa (NOAO/AURA/NSF)*
Compositor: *Lumina Datamatics, Inc.*

All credits appearing on page or at the end of the book are considered to be an extension of the copyright page.

Library of Congress Cataloging-in-Publication Data

Names: Rachels, Stuart, 1969- author. | Rachels, James, 1941-2003. Elements
    of moral philosophy.
Title: The elements of moral philosophy / James Rachels, editions 5-9 by
    Stuart Rachels.
Description: NINTH EDITION. | Dubuque, IA : McGraw-Hill Education, 2018. |
    Includes bibliographical references and index.
Identifiers: LCCN 2017059417 | ISBN 9781259914256 (pbk. : alk. paper)
Subjects: LCSH: Ethics—Textbooks.
Classification: LCC BJ1012 .R29 2018 | DDC 170—dc23 LC record available at
    https://lccn.loc.gov/2017059417

The Internet addresses listed in the text were accurate at the time of publication. The inclusion of a website does not indicate an endorsement by the authors or McGraw-Hill Education, and McGraw-Hill Education does not guarantee the accuracy of the information presented at these sites.

mheducation.com/highered

*A*bout the Authors

JAMES RACHELS (1941–2003) wrote *The End of Life: Euthanasia and Morality* (1986), *Created from Animals: The Moral Implications of Darwinism* (1990), *Can Ethics Provide Answers? And Other Essays in Moral Philosophy* (1997), *Problems from Philosophy* (first edition, 2005), and *The Legacy of Socrates: Essays in Moral Philosophy* (2007). His website is www.jamesrachels.org.

STUART RACHELS is Associate Professor of Philosophy at the University of Alabama. He has revised several of James Rachels' books, including *Problems from Philosophy* as well as the companion anthology to this book, *The Right Thing to Do*. Stuart won the U.S. Chess Championship in 1989, at the age of 20, and is a Bronze Life Master at bridge. He is currently writing a book about chess.

Contents

Preface

Socrates, one of the first and best moral philosophers, said that morality is about "no small matter, but how we ought to live." This book is an introduction to moral philosophy, conceived in that broad sense.

The field of ethics is immense. In the chapters that follow, I do not try to canvass every topic in the field, nor do I cover any topic comprehensively. Instead, I try to discuss the ideas that a newcomer to the subject should encounter first.

The chapters may be read independently of one another; they are, in effect, separate essays on separate topics. Thus, someone who is interested in Ethical Egoism could go straight to Chapter 5 and find a self-contained introduction to that theory. When read in order, however, the chapters tell a more or less continuous story. The first chapter presents a "minimum conception" of what morality is; the middle chapters cover the most important ethical theories; and the last chapter presents my own view of what a satisfactory moral theory would be like.

However, the point of this book is not to provide a neat, unified account of "the truth" about ethics. That would be a poor way to introduce the subject. Philosophy is not like physics. In physics, there is a large body of accepted truth that beginners must master. Of course, there are unresolved controversies in physics, but these take place against a backdrop of broad agreement. In philosophy, by contrast, everything is controversial—or almost everything. Some of the fundamental issues are still up for grabs. Newcomers to philosophy may ask themselves whether a moral theory such as Utilitarianism seems correct. However, newcomers to physics are rarely encouraged to make up their own minds about the laws of thermodynamics. A good introduction to ethics will not try to hide that somewhat embarrassing fact.

In these pages, you will find a survey of contending ideas, theories, and arguments. My own views, no doubt, color the presentation. I find some of these proposals more appealing than others, and a philosopher who made different assessments would no doubt write a different book. But I try to present the contending ideas fairly, and, when I pass judgment on an argument, I try to explain why. Philosophy, like morality itself, is first and last an exercise in reason; we should embrace the ideas, positions, and theories that our best arguments support.

*A*bout the Ninth Edition

In this edition, sex and drugs get more coverage. The section on same-sex relations (3.5) now discusses gay marriage, adoption rights, employment rights, Russia's "gay propaganda laws," teenage suicide, and hate crimes. The section on marijuana (7.3) now dips into the opioid crisis, the origins of the Drug War, the utilitarian rejection of "evil pleasures," the relationship between state law and federal law, and the harms of tobacco and alcohol abuse.

Here and there, the book has been updated to reflect recent events. For example, the concept of prejudice is now illustrated with a quotation from Donald Trump (5.4), and Mike Pence now represents opposition to gay rights (3.1). Some updates reflect a world that is increasingly online. For example, the importance of finding reliable sources of information is now discussed solely in terms of internet searches (1.5).

A few thoughts have been added to existing discussions. We now say that different societies may share some of the same values due to their shared human nature (at the end of 2.6), and we now qualify the claim that morality is "natural for human beings" on the grounds that morality may require humans to be unnaturally benevolent (13.1).

The initial explanation of the Principle of Utility now includes the phrase, "maximize happiness" (7.1). The dilemma in which absolute rules might conflict is now about a situation faced by doctors in New Orleans after Hurricane Katrina, instead of about Dutch fisherman having to lie during World War II (9.4).

Gone are Kurt Baier's argument that Ethical Egoism is logically inconsistent (from 5.4) and the examples of animal experimentation (from 7.4). I've also dropped the claim in Chapter 4 that Exodus 21 supports a liberal view of abortion, because I am no longer sure how to interpret that passage.

Finally, the age of the universe has been revised to reflect recent findings in astronomy (13.1).

For their help, I thank Caleb Andrews, Seth Bordner, Janice Daurio, Micah Davis, Daniel Hollingshead, Kaave Lajevardi, Cayce Moore, Howard Pospesel, John Rowell, Mike Vincke, and Chase Wrenn. My biggest thanks go to my wife, Professor Heather Elliott, and to my mother, Carol Rachels, for their tremendous help down the stretch.

My father, James Rachels, wrote the first four editions of *The Elements of Moral Philosophy*. It is still his book.

—Stuart Rachels

 **connect**®

McGraw-Hill Connect® is a highly reliable, easy-to-use homework and learning management solution that utilizes learning science and award-winning adaptive tools to improve student results.

Homework and Adaptive Learning

- Connect's assignments help students contextualize what they've learned through application, so they can better understand the material and think critically.
- Connect will create a personalized study path customized to individual student needs through SmartBook®.
- SmartBook helps students study more efficiently by delivering an interactive reading experience through adaptive highlighting and review.

Connect's Impact on Retention Rates, Pass Rates, and Average Exam Scores

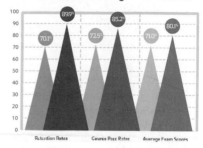

Retention Rates: without Connect 70.1%, with Connect 89.9%
Course Pass Rates: without Connect 72.5%, with Connect 86.2%
Average Exam Scores: without Connect 71.0%, with Connect 80.1%

■ without Connect   ■ with Connect

Over **7 billion questions** have been answered, making McGraw-Hill Education products more intelligent, reliable, and precise.

Using **Connect** improves retention rates by **19.8%**, passing rates by **12.7%**, and exam scores by **9.1%**.

73% of instructors who use **Connect** require it; instructor satisfaction **increases** by 28% when **Connect** is required.

Quality Content and Learning Resources

- Connect content is authored by the world's best subject matter experts, and is available to your class through a simple and intuitive interface.
- The Connect eBook makes it easy for students to access their reading material on smartphones and tablets. They can study on the go and don't need internet access to use the eBook as a reference, with full functionality.
- Multimedia content such as videos, simulations, and games drive student engagement and critical thinking skills.

Robust Analytics and Reporting

- Connect Insight® generates easy-to-read reports on individual students, the class as a whole, and on specific assignments.
- The Connect Insight dashboard delivers data on performance, study behavior, and effort. Instructors can quickly identify students who struggle and focus on material that the class has yet to master.
- Connect automatically grades assignments and quizzes, providing easy-to-read reports on individual and class performance.

©Hero Images/Getty Images

Impact on Final Course Grade Distribution

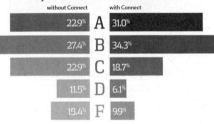

without Connect		with Connect
22.9%	A	31.0%
27.4%	B	34.3%
22.9%	C	18.7%
11.5%	D	6.1%
15.4%	F	9.9%

More students earn **As** and **Bs** when they use **Connect**.

Trusted Service and Support

- Connect integrates with your LMS to provide single sign-on and automatic syncing of grades. Integration with Blackboard®, D2L®, and Canvas also provides automatic syncing of the course calendar and assignment-level linking.
- Connect offers comprehensive service, support, and training throughout every phase of your implementation.
- If you're looking for some guidance on how to use Connect, or want to learn tips and tricks from super users, you can find tutorials as you work. Our Digital Faculty Consultants and Student Ambassadors offer insight into how to achieve the results you want with Connect.

www.mheducation.com/connect

CHAPTER 1

What Is Morality?

We are discussing no small matter, but how we ought to live.
SOCRATES, IN PLATO'S *REPUBLIC* (ca. 390 B.C.)

1.1. The Problem of Definition

Moral philosophy is the study of what morality is and what it requires of us. As Socrates said, it's about "how we ought to live"— and why. It would be helpful if we could begin with a simple, uncontroversial definition of what morality is. Unfortunately, we cannot. There are many rival theories, each expounding a different conception of what it means to live morally, and any definition that goes beyond Socrates's simple formulation is bound to offend at least one of them.

This should make us cautious, but it need not paralyze us. In this chapter, I will describe the "minimum conception" of morality. As the name suggests, the minimum conception is a core that every moral theory should accept, at least as a starting point. First, however, we will examine some moral controversies having to do with handicapped children. This discussion will bring out the features of the minimum conception.

1.2. First Example: Baby Theresa

Theresa Ann Campo Pearson, an infant known to the public as "Baby Theresa," was born in Florida in 1992. Baby Theresa had anencephaly, one of the worst genetic disorders. Anencephalic infants are sometimes referred to as "babies without brains," but that is not quite accurate. Important parts of the brain—the cerebrum and cerebellum—are missing, as is the top of the skull. The brain stem, however, is still there, and so the baby can breathe and possess a heartbeat. In the United States, most cases of anencephaly are detected during pregnancy, and the fetuses are usually aborted. Of those not aborted, half are stillborn. Of those born alive, most die within days.

Baby Theresa's story is remarkable only because her parents made an unusual request. Knowing that their baby would die soon and could never be conscious, Theresa's parents volunteered her organs for immediate transplant. They thought that her kidneys, liver, heart, lungs, and eyes should go to other children who could benefit from them. Her physicians agreed. Thousands of infants need transplants each year, and there are never enough organs available. However, Theresa's organs were not taken, because Florida law forbids the removal of organs until the donor has died. And by the time Baby Theresa died, nine days later, it was too late—her organs had deteriorated too much to be transplanted.

Baby Theresa's case was widely debated. Should she have been killed so that her organs could have been used to save other children? A number of professional "ethicists"—people who get paid by universities, hospitals, and law schools to think about such things—were asked by the press to comment. Most of them disagreed with the parents, instead appealing to time-honored philosophical principles. "It just seems too horrifying to use people as means to other people's ends," said one such expert. Another explained: "It's unethical to kill person A to save person B." And a third added: "What the parents are really asking for is, Kill this dying baby so that its organs may be used for someone else. Well, that's really a horrendous proposition."

Is it horrendous? Opinions were divided. These ethicists thought it was, while the parents and doctors did not. But we are interested in more than what people happen to believe. We want to know what's true. Were the parents right or wrong to volunteer their baby's organs for transplant? To answer this question, we have to ask what reasons, or arguments, can be given on each side. What can be said for or against the parents' request?

The Benefits Argument. The parents believed that Theresa's organs were doing her no good, because she was not conscious and was bound to die soon. The other children, however, could be helped. Thus, the parents seem to have reasoned: *If we can benefit someone without harming anyone else, then we ought to do so. Transplanting the organs would benefit the other children without harming Baby Theresa. Therefore, we ought to transplant the organs.*

Is this correct? Not every argument is sound. In addition to knowing what arguments can be given for a view, we also want to know whether those arguments are any good. Generally speaking, an argument is sound if its assumptions are true and the conclusion follows logically from them. In this case, the argument has two assumptions: that we should help someone if no harm would come of it, and that the transplant would help the other children without harming Theresa. We might wonder, however, about the claim that Theresa wouldn't be harmed. After all, she would die, and wouldn't dying be bad for her? Yet on reflection, it seems clear that the parents were right, under these tragic circumstances. Staying alive is good for someone only if it allows her to do things and to have thoughts and feelings and relations with other people—in other words, only if the individual who is alive *has a life*. Without such things, mere biological existence has no value. Therefore, even though Theresa might remain alive for a few more days, it would do her no good.

The Benefits Argument provides a powerful reason for transplanting the organs. What arguments exist on the other side?

The Argument That We Should Not Use People as Means. The ethicists who opposed the transplants offered two arguments. The first was based on the idea that *it is wrong to use people as means to other people's goals.* Taking Theresa's organs would be using her to benefit the other children, whom she doesn't know and cares nothing about; therefore, it should not be done.

Is this argument sound? The idea that we should not "use" people is appealing, but this idea is vague. What exactly does it mean? "Using people" typically involves violating their *autonomy*—their ability to decide for themselves how to live their own lives, based on their own desires and values. A person's autonomy may be violated through manipulation, trickery, or deceit. For example, I may pretend to be your friend, when I am only interested in going out with your sister; or I may lie to you, so you'll give me money; or I may try to convince you that you would enjoy going to a movie, when, really, I only want you to give me a ride. In each case, I am manipulating you in order to get something for myself. Autonomy is also violated when people are forced to do things against their will. This explains why "using people" is wrong; it is wrong because it thwarts their autonomy.

Taking Baby Theresa's organs, however, could not thwart her autonomy, because she has no autonomy—she cannot make decisions, she has no desires, and she cannot value anything. Would taking her organs be "using her" in any other morally significant sense? We would, of course, be using her organs for someone else's benefit. But we do that every time we perform a transplant. We would also be using her organs without her permission. Would that make it wrong? If we were using them *against* her wishes, then that would be a reason for objecting— it would violate her autonomy. But Baby Theresa has no wishes.

When people are unable to make decisions for themselves, and others must step in, there are two reasonable guidelines that might be adopted. First, we might ask, *What would be in their own best interests?* If we apply this standard to Baby Theresa, there would be no problem with taking her organs, for, as we have already noted, her interests will not be affected. She is not conscious, and she will die soon no matter what.

The second guideline appeals to the person's own preferences: We might ask, *If she could tell us what she wants, what would she say?* This sort of thought is useful when we are dealing with people who have preferences (or once had them) but cannot express them—for example, a comatose patient who signed a living will before slipping into the coma. But, sadly, Baby Theresa has no preferences, nor can she ever have any. So we can get no guidance from her, not even in our imaginations. The upshot is that we are left to do what we think is best.

The Argument from the Wrongness of Killing. The ethicists also appealed to the principle that *it is wrong to kill one person to save another.* Taking Theresa's organs would be killing her to save others, they said; so, taking the organs would be wrong.

Is this argument sound? The rule against killing is certainly among the most important moral precepts. Nevertheless, few people believe it is *always* wrong to kill—most people think there are exceptions, such as killing in self-defense. The question, then, is whether taking Baby Theresa's organs should be regarded as another exception. There are many reasons to think so: Baby Theresa is not conscious; she will never have a life; she is bound to die soon; and taking her organs would help the other babies. Anyone who accepts this will regard the argument as flawed. Usually, it is wrong to kill one person to save another, but not always.

There is another possibility. Perhaps we should regard Baby Theresa as already dead. If this sounds crazy, bear in mind that our conception of death has changed over the years. In 1967, the South African doctor Christiaan Barnard performed the first heart transplant in a human being. This was an exciting development; heart transplants could potentially save many lives. It was not clear, however, whether any lives could be saved in the United States. Back then, American law understood death as occurring when the heart stops beating. But once a heart stops beating, the organ quickly degrades and becomes unsuitable for transplant. Thus, under American law, it was not clear whether any hearts could be harvested for transplant. So American law changed. We now understand death as occurring, not when the heart stops beating, but when the brain stops functioning: "brain death" is now our standard understanding of death. This solved the problem about transplants because a brain-dead patient can still have a healthy heart, suitable for transplant.

Anencephalics do not meet the technical requirements for brain death as that term is currently defined, but perhaps the definition should be revised to include them. After all, they lack any hope for conscious life, because they have no cerebrum or cerebellum. If the definition of brain death were reformulated to include anencephalics, then we would become accustomed to the idea that these unfortunate infants are stillborn, and so taking their organs would not involve killing them. The Argument from the Wrongness of Killing would then be moot.

On the whole, then, the arguments in favor of transplanting Baby Theresa's organs seem stronger than the arguments against it.

1.3. Second Example: Jodie and Mary

In August 2000, a young woman from Gozo, an island south of Italy, discovered that she was carrying conjoined twins. Knowing that the health-care facilities on Gozo couldn't handle such a birth, she and her husband went to St. Mary's Hospital in Manchester, England.

The infants, known as Mary and Jodie, were joined at the lower abdomen. Their spines were fused, and they had one heart and one pair of lungs between them. Jodie, the stronger one, was providing blood for her sister.

No one knows how many conjoined twins are born each year, but the number seems to be in the hundreds. Most die shortly after birth, but some do well. They grow to adulthood and marry and have children themselves. However, the outlook for Mary and Jodie was grim. The doctors said that, without intervention, the girls would die within six months. The only hope was an operation to separate them. This would save Jodie, but Mary would die immediately.

The parents, who were devout Catholics, opposed the operation on the grounds that it would hasten Mary's death. "We believe that nature should take its course," they said. "If it's God's will that both our children should not survive, then so be it." The hospital, hoping to save Jodie, petitioned the courts for permission to perform the operation anyway. The courts agreed, and the operation was performed. As expected, Jodie lived and Mary died.

In thinking about this case, we should distinguish the question of *who should make the decision* from the question of *what the decision should be*. You might think, for example, that the parents should make the decision, and so the courts were wrong to intrude. But there remains the question of what would be the wisest choice for the parents (or anyone else) to make. We will focus on that question: Was it right or wrong to separate the twins?

The Argument That We Should Save as Many as We Can. The rationale for separating the twins is that we have a choice between saving one infant or letting both die. Isn't it plainly better to save one? This argument is so appealing that many people will conclude, without further thought, that the twins should be separated. At the height of the controversy, the *Ladies' Home Journal* commissioned a poll to discover what Americans thought. The poll showed that 78% approved of the operation. People were persuaded by the idea that we should save as many as we can. Jodie and Mary's parents, however, were persuaded by a different argument.

The Argument from the Sanctity of Human Life. The parents loved both of their children, and they thought it would be wrong to kill one of them even to save the other. Of course, they were not alone in thinking this. The idea that all human life is precious, regardless of age, race, social class, or handicap, is at the core of the Western moral tradition. In traditional ethics, the rule against killing innocent humans is absolute. It does not matter if the killing would serve a good purpose; it simply cannot be done. Mary is an innocent human being, and so she may not be killed.

Is this argument sound? The judges who heard the case did not think so, for a surprising reason. They denied that the operation would kill Mary. Lord Justice Robert Walker said that the operation would merely separate Mary from her sister and then "she would die, not because she was intentionally killed, but because her own body cannot sustain her life." In other words, the operation wouldn't kill her; her body's weakness would. And so, the morality of killing is irrelevant.

This response, however, misses the point. It doesn't matter whether we say that Mary's death was caused by the operation, or by the weakness of her own body. Either way, she will be dead, and we would knowingly have hastened her death. *That's* the idea behind the traditional ban on killing the innocent.

There is, however, a more natural objection to the Argument from the Sanctity of Human Life. Perhaps it is *not* always wrong to kill innocent human beings. For example, such killings might be right when three conditions are met: (a) the innocent human has no future because she must die soon no matter what; (b) the innocent human has no wish to go on living, perhaps because she has no wishes at all; and (c) this killing will save others, who can go on to lead full lives. In these rare circumstances, the killing of the innocent might be justified.

1.4. Third Example: Tracy Latimer

Tracy Latimer, a 12-year-old victim of cerebral palsy, was killed by her father in 1993. Tracy lived with her family on a prairie farm in Saskatchewan, Canada. One Sunday morning while his wife and other children were at church, Robert Latimer put Tracy in the cab of his pickup truck and piped in exhaust fumes until she died. At the time of her death, Tracy weighed less than 40 pounds, and she was described as "functioning at the mental level of a three-month-old baby." Mrs. Latimer said that she was relieved to find Tracy dead when she arrived home. She said she "didn't have the courage" to do it herself.

Robert Latimer was tried for murder, but the judge and jury did not want to punish him severely. The jury found him guilty of only second-degree murder and recommended that the judge ignore the 10-year sentence that is mandatory for such a crime. The judge agreed and sentenced him to one year in prison, followed by one year of confinement to his farm. But the Supreme Court of Canada stepped in and ruled that the mandatory sentence must be imposed. Robert Latimer entered prison in 2001 and was released on parole in 2008.

Legal questions aside, did Mr. Latimer do anything wrong? This case involves many of the issues that we saw in the other cases. One argument is that Tracy's life was morally precious, and so her father had no right to kill her. But in his defense, it may be said that Tracy's condition was so catastrophic that she had no prospects of a "life" in any but the merest biological sense. Her existence consisted in pointless suffering, and so killing her was an act of mercy. Considering those arguments, it appears that Robert Latimer acted defensibly. His critics, however, made other points.

The Argument from the Wrongness of Discriminating against the Handicapped. When the trial court gave Robert Latimer a light sentence, many handicapped people felt insulted. The president of the Saskatoon Voice of People with Disabilities, who has multiple sclerosis, said, "Nobody has the right to decide my life is worth less than yours. That's the bottom line." Tracy was killed because she was handicapped, he said, and that is immoral. Handicapped people should be given the same respect and accorded the same rights as everyone else.

What are we to make of this? Discrimination is always a serious matter, because it involves treating some people worse than others, for no good reason. Suppose, for example, that a blind person is turned down for a job simply because the employer doesn't want to be around someone who can't see. This is no better than refusing to hire someone because she is Hispanic or Jewish or female. Why is this person treated differently? Is she less able to do the job? Is she less intelligent or less hardworking? Does she deserve the job less? Is she less able to benefit from being employed? If there is no good reason to exclude her, then it is wrong to do so.

Was Tracy Latimer's death a case of discrimination against the handicapped? Robert Latimer argued that Tracy's cerebral palsy was not the issue: "People are saying this is a handicap issue, but they're wrong. This is a torture issue. It was about mutilation and torture for Tracy." Just before her death, Tracy had undergone major surgery on her back, hips, and legs, and more surgery was planned. "With the combination of a feeding tube, rods in her back, the leg cut and flopping around and bedsores," said her father, "how can people say she was a happy little girl?" At the trial, three of Tracy's physicians testified about the difficulty of controlling her pain. Thus, Mr. Latimer denied that Tracy was killed because of her disability; she was killed because she was suffering without hope of relief.

The Slippery Slope Argument. When the Canadian Supreme Court upheld Robert Latimer's long, mandatory sentence, the director of the Canadian Association of Independent Living Centres was pleasantly surprised. "It would have really been the slippery slope, and opening the doors to other people to decide who should live and who should die," she said.

Other disability advocates agreed. We may feel sympathy for Robert Latimer, they said; we may even think that Tracy Latimer is better off dead. However, it is dangerous to think in this way. If we accept any sort of mercy killing, they said, we will slide down a "slippery slope," and at the bottom of the slope, all life will be held cheap. Where will we draw the line? If Tracy's life is not worth protecting, what about the lives of other disabled people? What about the elderly, the infirm, and other "useless" members of society? In this context, Adolf Hitler's program of "racial purification" may be mentioned, implying that we will become like the Nazis if we take the first step.

Similar "slippery slope arguments" have been used on other issues. Abortion, in vitro fertilization (IVF), and human cloning have all been denounced because of what they might lead to. In hindsight, it is sometimes obvious that the worries were unfounded. This has happened with IVF, a technique for creating embryos in the lab. When Louise Brown, the first "test tube baby," was born in 1978, there were dire predictions about what this might mean for the future of our species. However, nothing awful happened, and IVF has become a routine procedure.

Without the benefit of hindsight, however, slippery slope arguments are often tough to assess. As the old saying goes, "It's hard to make predictions, especially about the future." Reasonable people may disagree about what would happen if mercy killing were allowed in cases like Tracy Latimer's. People who want to condemn Mr. Latimer may see disaster looming, while those who support Mr. Latimer may have no such worries.

It is worth noting that slippery slope arguments are easy to abuse. If you are opposed to something but can't think of a good reason why, then you can always dream up something terrible that might happen as a result of that thing; and no matter how unrealistic your prediction is, no one can prove you wrong. That is why we should approach such arguments with caution.

1.5. Reason and Impartiality

What can we learn from these cases about the nature of morality? For starters, we may note two points: first, moral judgments must be backed by good reasons; and second, morality requires the impartial consideration of each individual's interests.

Moral Reasoning. The cases of Baby Theresa, Jodie and Mary, and Tracy Latimer may arouse strong feelings in us. Such feelings might be admirable; they might be a sign of moral seriousness. However, they can also get in the way of discovering the truth. When we feel strongly about an issue, it is tempting to assume that we simply *know* what the truth is, without even having to consider the arguments. Unfortunately, however, we cannot rely on our feelings. Our feelings may be irrational; they may be due to prejudice, selfishness, or cultural conditioning. At one time, for example, many people's feelings told them that members of other races were inferior and that slavery was part of God's great plan.

Also, people's feelings vary. In the case of Tracy Latimer, some people feel strongly that her father deserved a long prison term; other people support the father passionately. But both of these feelings cannot be correct. If we assume that our view must be correct, simply because *we* hold it, then we are just being arrogant.

Thus, if we want to discover the truth, we must let our feelings be guided as much as possible by reason. This is the essence of morality. The morally right thing to do is always the thing best supported by the arguments.

This is not a narrow point about a small range of moral views; it is a general requirement of logic. The fundamental point is this: If someone says that you ought to do such-and-such, then you may legitimately ask why; and if no good reason can be given, then you may reject the advice as arbitrary or unfounded.

In this way, moral judgments are different from expressions of personal taste. If someone says, "I like the taste of coffee," she doesn't need to have a reason—she is merely stating her preferences. There is no such thing as "rationally defending" one's like of coffee. On the other hand, if someone says that something is morally wrong, then he *does* need reasons; and if his reasons are legitimate, then other people should agree with him. By the same logic, if he has no good reason for what he says, then he is simply making noise and may be ignored.

But how can we figure out whether a reason is good? How can we assess moral arguments? The examples we have considered point to some answers.

The first thing is to get your facts straight. This may not be easy. Sometimes you might *want* something to be true, and so your "investigation" of it is unreliable. If all you do is surf the web, looking to confirm what you already believe, then you will always succeed. Yet the facts exist apart from our wishes. We need to see the world as it is, not as we want it to be. Thus, in seeking information, you should try to find reliable, informed sources instead of, say, typing what you believe into Google and then looking for websites that say the same thing.

Even when our investigation is unbiased, we might still be unsure of some things. Sometimes, a key fact is simply unknown; and sometimes, an issue is so complex that even the experts disagree about it. However, we have to do the best we can.

Next, we can bring moral principles into play. In this chapter, we have considered a number of principles: that we should not "use" people; that we should not kill one person to save another; that we should do what will benefit people; that every life is sacred; and that it is wrong to discriminate against the handicapped. Most moral arguments consist of applying principles to particular cases, and so we must ask whether the principles are justified and whether they are being applied correctly.

It would be nice if there were a simple recipe for constructing good arguments and avoiding bad ones. Unfortunately, there is not. Arguments can go wrong in many ways, and we might always encounter a new kind of error. Yet this should not surprise us. The rote application of routine methods is no replacement for critical thinking.

The Requirement of Impartiality. Almost every important moral theory includes a commitment to impartiality. To be impartial is to treat everyone alike; no one gets special treatment. By contrast, to be partial is to show favoritism. Impartiality also requires that we not treat the members of particular *groups* as inferior. Thus it condemns forms of discrimination like sexism and racism.

Impartiality is closely tied to the idea that moral judgments must be backed by good reasons. Consider the racist who thinks that white people should get all the good jobs. He wants all the doctors, lawyers, business executives, and so on to be white. Now we can ask him for reasons; we can ask him why. Is there something about white people that makes them better fitted for the highest-paying and most prestigious jobs? Are they inherently brighter or harder working? Do they care more about themselves and their families? Would they benefit more from having the jobs? In each case, the answer is no; and if there is no good reason to treat people differently, then to do so is unacceptably arbitrary; it is discrimination.

The requirement of impartiality, then, is at bottom nothing more than a rule against treating people arbitrarily. It forbids treating one person worse than another when there is no good reason to do so. Yet if this explains why racism is wrong, it also explains why some cases of unequal treatment are *not* racist. Suppose a movie director were making a film about Fred Shuttlesworth (1922–2011), the heroic African-American civil rights leader. This director would have a good reason not to cast Chris Pratt in the starring role—namely, that Pratt is white. Such a decision would not be arbitrary or objectionable; it would not be discrimination.

1.6. The Minimum Conception of Morality

We may now state the minimum conception: Morality is, at the very least, the effort to guide one's conduct by reason—that is, to do what there are the best reasons for doing—while giving equal weight to the interests of each individual affected by one's action.

This paints a picture of what it means to be a conscientious moral agent. The conscientious moral agent is someone who is concerned impartially with the interests of everyone affected by what he or she does; who carefully sifts facts and examines their implications; who accepts principles of conduct only after scrutinizing them to make sure they are justified; who will "listen to reason" even when it means revising prior convictions; and who, finally, is willing to act on these deliberations.

As one might expect, not every ethical theory accepts this "minimum." This picture of the conscientious moral agent has been disputed in various ways. However, theories that reject it encounter serious difficulties. This is why most moral theories embrace the minimum conception, in one form or another.

Notes on Sources

The ethicists' comments about Baby Theresa are from an Associated Press report: David Briggs, "Baby Theresa Case Raises Ethics Questions," *Champaign-Urbana News-Gazette*, March 31, 1992, p. A-6.

For information on conjoined twins, see the University of Maryland Medical Center website: http://umm.edu/programs/conjoined-twins/facts-about-the-twins.

The poll about separating conjoined twins is from the *Ladies' Home Journal*, March 2001. The judges' comments about Jodie and Mary are from the *Daily Telegraph*, September 23, 2000.

Information about Tracy Latimer is from *The New York Times*, December 1, 1997, National Edition, p. A-3.

CHAPTER 2

The Challenge of Cultural Relativism

Morality differs in every society, and is a convenient term for socially
approved habits.

RUTH BENEDICT, *PATTERNS OF CULTURE* (1934)

2.1. Different Cultures Have Different Moral Codes

Darius, a king of ancient Persia (present-day Iran), was intrigued by
the variety of cultures he met in his travels. In India, for example,
he had encountered a group of people known as the Callatians who
cooked and ate the bodies of their dead fathers. The Greeks, of
course, did not do that—they practiced cremation and regarded the
funeral pyre as the proper way to dispose of the dead. Darius thought
that an enlightened outlook should appreciate such differences. One
day, to teach this lesson, he summoned some Greeks who were at
his court and asked them what it would take for them to eat their
dead fathers' bodies. The Greeks were shocked, as Darius knew they
would be. No amount of money, they said, could possibly get them
to do such a thing. Then Darius called in some Callatians and, while
the Greeks listened, asked if they would be willing to burn their dead
fathers' bodies. The Callatians were horrified and told Darius not
to speak of such things.

This story, recounted by Herodotus in his *History*, illustrates a
recurring theme in the literature of social science: Different cultures
have different moral codes. What is thought to be right within one
group may horrify another group, and vice versa. Should we eat the

bodies of our dead or burn them? If you were Greek, one answer would seem obviously correct; but if you were Callatian, then the other answer would seem certain.

There are many examples of this. Consider the Eskimos of the early and mid-20th century. The Eskimos are the native people of Alaska, northern Canada, Greenland, and northeastern Siberia, in Asiatic Russia. Today, none of these groups call themselves "Eskimos," but the term has historically referred to that scattered Arctic population. Prior to the 20th century, the outside world knew little about them. Then explorers began to bring back strange tales.

The Eskimos lived in small settlements, separated by great distances, and their customs turned out to be very different from ours. The men often had more than one wife, and they would share their wives with guests, lending them out for the night as a sign of hospitality. Within a community, a dominant male might demand—and get—regular sexual access to other men's wives. The women, however, were free to break these arrangements simply by leaving their husbands and taking up with new partners—free, that is, insofar as their former husbands did not make too much trouble. All in all, the Eskimo custom of marriage was a volatile practice, very unlike our own custom.

But it was not only their marriages and sexual practices that were different. The Eskimos also seemed to care less about human life. Infanticide, for example, was common. Knud Rasmussen, an early explorer, reported meeting a woman who had borne 20 children but had killed 10 of them at birth. Female babies, he found, were killed more often than males, and this was allowed at the parents' discretion, with no social stigma attached. Moreover, when elderly family members became too feeble, they were left out in the snow to die.

Most of us would find these Eskimo customs completely unacceptable. Our own way of living seems so natural and right to us that we can hardly conceive of people who live so differently. When we hear of such people, we might think of them as being "backward" or "primitive." But to anthropologists, the Eskimos did not seem unusual. Since the time of Herodotus, enlightened observers have known that conceptions of right and wrong differ from culture to culture. If we assume that everyone shares our values, then we are merely being naïve.

2.2. Cultural Relativism

To many people, this observation—"Different cultures have different moral codes"—seems like the key to understanding morality. There are no universal moral truths, they say; the customs of different societies are all that exist. To call a custom "correct" or "incorrect" would imply that we can judge it by some independent or objective standard of right and wrong. But, in fact, we would merely be judging it by the standards of our own culture. No *independent* standard exists; every standard is culture-bound. The sociologist William Graham Sumner (1840–1910) put it like this:

> The "right" way is the way which the ancestors used and which has been handed down. . . . The notion of right is in the folk-ways. It is not outside of them, of independent origin, and brought to test them. In the folkways, whatever is, is right. This is because they are traditional, and therefore contain in themselves the authority of the ancestral ghosts. When we come to the folkways we are at the end of our analysis.

This line of thought, more than any other, has persuaded people to be skeptical about ethics. Cultural Relativism says, in effect, that there is no such thing as universal truth in ethics; there are only the various cultural codes. Cultural Relativism challenges our belief in the objectivity and legitimacy of moral judgments.

The following claims have all been emphasized by cultural relativists:

1. Different societies have different moral codes.
2. The moral code of a society determines what is right within that society; so, if a society says that a certain action is right, then that action *is* right, at least in that society.
3. There is no objective standard that can be used to judge one society's code as better than another's. There are no moral truths that hold for all people at all times.

4. The moral code of our own society has no special status; it is but one among many.
5. It is arrogant for us to judge other cultures. We should always be tolerant of them.

The second claim—that right and wrong are determined by the norms of society—is at the heart of Cultural Relativism. However, it may seem to conflict with the fifth claim, which is that we should always be tolerant of other cultures. Should we *always* tolerate them? What if the norms of our society favor *not* tolerating them? For example, when the Nazi army invaded Poland on September 1, 1939, thus beginning World War II, this was an intolerant action of the first order. But what if it conformed to Nazi ideals? A cultural relativist, it seems, cannot criticize the Nazis for being intolerant, if all they're doing is following their own moral beliefs.

Given that cultural relativists take pride in their tolerance, it would be ironic if their theory actually supported the intolerance of warlike societies. However, their theory need not do that. Properly understood, Cultural Relativism holds that the norms of a culture reign supreme *within the bounds of the culture itself*. Once the German soldiers entered Poland, they became bound by the norms of Polish society—norms that obviously excluded the mass slaughter of innocent Poles. "When in Rome," the old saying goes, "do as the Romans do." Cultural relativists agree.

2.3. The Cultural Differences Argument

Cultural Relativists often make a certain type of argument. They begin with facts about cultures and wind up drawing a conclusion about morality. For example, they invite us to accept this reasoning:

(1) The Greeks believed it was wrong to eat the dead, whereas the Callatians believed it was right to eat the dead.

(2) Therefore, eating the dead is neither objectively right nor objectively wrong. It is merely a matter of opinion, which varies from culture to culture.

Or:

(1) The Eskimos saw nothing wrong with infanticide, whereas Americans believe that infanticide is immoral.

(2) Therefore, infanticide is neither objectively right nor objectively wrong. It is merely a matter of opinion, which varies from culture to culture.

Clearly, these arguments are variations of one fundamental idea. They are both examples of a more general argument, which says:

(1) Different cultures have different moral codes.

(2) Therefore, there is no objective truth in morality. Right and wrong are only matters of opinion, and opinions vary from culture to culture.

Let's call this the *Cultural Differences Argument*. To many people, it is persuasive. But is it a good argument—is it sound?

It is not. For an argument to be *sound*, its premises must all be true, and its conclusion must logically *follow from* them. Here, the problem is that the conclusion does not follow from the premise—that is, even if the premise is true, the conclusion might still be false. The premise concerns what people *believe*—in some societies, people believe one thing; in other societies, people believe something else. The conclusion, however, concerns what *really is the case*. This sort of conclusion does not follow logically from that sort of premise. In philosophical terminology, this means that the argument is *invalid*.

Consider again the example of the Greeks and Callatians. The Greeks believed it was wrong to eat the dead; the Callatians believed it was right. Does it follow, *from the mere fact that they disagreed*, that there is no objective truth in the matter? No, it does not; there might be an objective truth that neither party sees, or a truth that *only one party* sees.

To make the point clearer, consider a different matter. In some societies, people believe the earth is flat. In other societies, such as our own, people believe that the earth is a sphere. Does it follow, from the mere fact that people disagree, that there is no "objective truth" in geography? Of course not; we would never draw such a conclusion, because we realize that the members of some societies might simply be wrong. Even if the world is round, some people might not know it. Similarly, there might be some moral truths that are not universally known. The Cultural Differences Argument tries to derive a moral conclusion from the mere fact that people disagree. But this is impossible.

This point should not be misunderstood. We are not saying that the conclusion of the argument is false; for all we have said, it could still be true. The point is that the Cultural Differences Argument *does not prove* that it is true. Rather, the argument fails.

2.4. What Follows from Cultural Relativism

If Cultural Relativism were true, then what would follow from it?

In the passage quoted earlier, William Graham Sumner states the essence of Cultural Relativism. He says that the only measure of right and wrong is the standards of one's society: "The notion of right is in the folkways. It is not outside of them, of independent origin, and brought to test them. In the folkways, whatever is, is right." Suppose we took this seriously. What would be some of the consequences?

1. *We could no longer say that the customs of other societies are morally inferior to our own.* This is one of the main points stressed by Cultural Relativism—that we should never condemn a society merely because it is "different." This attitude seems enlightened, especially when we concentrate on examples like the funerary practices of the Greeks and Callatians.

However, if Cultural Relativism were true, then we would also be barred from criticizing other, more harmful practices. For example, the Chinese government has a long history of repressing political dissent within its own borders. At any given time, thousands of prisoners in China are doing hard labor on account of their political views, and in the Tiananmen Square episode of 1989, Chinese troops slaughtered hundreds, if not thousands, of peaceful protesters. Cultural Relativism would prevent us from saying that the Chinese government's policies of oppression are wrong. We could not even say that respect for free speech is *better* than the Chinese practice, for that too would imply a universal or objective standard of comparison. However, refusing to condemn *these* practices does not seem enlightened; on the contrary, political oppression seems wrong wherever it occurs. Yet if we accept Cultural Relativism, then we have to regard such practices as immune from criticism.

2. *We could no longer criticize the code of our own society.* Cultural Relativism suggests a simple test for determining what is right and what is wrong: All we need to do is ask whether the action is in line with the code of the society in which it occurs. Suppose a resident of India wonders whether her country's caste system—a system of rigid social hierarchy—is morally correct. All she has to do is ask whether this system conforms to her society's moral code. If it does, then there is no way it can be wrong.

This implication of Cultural Relativism is disturbing because few of us think that our society's code is perfect. Rather, we can think of ways in which it might be improved. We can also think of ways in which we might learn from other cultures. Yet Cultural Relativism stops us from criticizing our own society's code, and it bars us from seeing ways in which other cultures might be better. After all, if right and wrong are relative to culture, this must be true for our own culture, just as it is for other cultures.

3. *The idea of moral progress is called into doubt.* We think that at least some social changes are for the better. For example, through-out most of Western history, the place of women in society was narrowly defined. Women could not own property; they could not vote or hold political office; and they were under the almost absolute control of their husbands or fathers. Recently, much of this has changed, and most of us think of this as progress.

But if Cultural Relativism is correct, can we legitimately view this as progress? Progress means replacing the old ways with new and improved ways. But by what standard can a Cultural Relativist judge the new ways as *better*? If the old ways conformed to the standards of their time, then Cultural Relativists could not condemn them. After all, those old ways or traditions "had their own time and place," and we should not judge *them* by *our* standards. Sexist 19th-century society was a different society from the one we now inhabit. Thus, a Cultural Relativist could not regard the progress that women have made over the centuries as being (real) progress— after all, to speak of "real progress" is to make just the sort of transcultural judgment that Cultural Relativism forbids.

According to Cultural Relativism, there is only one way to improve a society: to make it better match its own ideals. After all, those ideals will determine whether progress has been made. No one, however, may challenge the ideals themselves. According to Cultural Relativism, then, the idea of social reform makes sense only in this limited way.

These three consequences of Cultural Relativism have led many people to reject it. To take another example, we all want to condemn slavery wherever it occurs, and we all believe that the widespread abolition of slavery in the Western world was a mark of human progress. Because Cultural Relativism disagrees, it cannot be correct.

2.5. Why There Is Less Disagreement Than There Seems to Be

Cultural Relativism starts by observing that cultures differ dramatically in their views of right and wrong. But how much do they really differ? It is true that there are differences, but it is easy to exaggerate them. Often, what seems at first to be a big difference turns out to be no difference at all.

Consider a culture in which people condemn eating cows. This may even be a poor culture, in which there is not enough food; still, the cows are not to be touched. Such a society would appear to have values very different from our own. But does it? We have not yet asked *why* these folks won't eat cows. Suppose they believe that, after death, the souls of humans inhabit the bodies of other types of animals, especially cows, so that a cow could be someone's grandmother. Shall we say that their values differ from ours? No; the difference lies elsewhere. We differ in our beliefs, not in our values. We agree that we shouldn't eat Grandma; we disagree about whether the cow might be Grandma.

The point is that many factors work together to produce the customs of a society. Not only are the society's values important but so are its religious beliefs, its factual beliefs, and its physical environment. Thus, we cannot conclude that two societies differ in values just because they differ in customs. After all, customs may differ for a number of reasons. Thus, there may be less moral disagreement across cultures than there appears to be.

Consider again the Eskimos, who killed healthy infants, especially infant girls. We do not approve of such things; in our society, a parent who kills a baby will be locked up. Thus, there appears to be a great difference in the values of our two cultures. But suppose we ask why the Eskimos did this. The explanation is not that they lacked respect for human life or that they did not love their children. An Eskimo family would always protect its babies if conditions permitted. But the Eskimos lived in a harsh environment, where food was scarce. To quote an old Eskimo saying: "Life is hard, and the margin of safety small." A family may want to nourish its babies but be unable to do so.

Several factors, in addition to the lack of food, explain why the Eskimos sometimes resorted to infanticide. For one thing, they lacked birth control, and so unwanted pregnancies were common. Another fact is that Eskimo mothers would typically nurse their infants over a much longer period than do mothers in our culture—for four years, and sometimes even longer. So, even in the best of times, one mother could sustain very few children. Moreover, the Eskimos were nomadic; unable to farm in the harsh arctic climate, they had to keep moving to find food. Infants had to be carried, and a mother could carry only one baby in her parka as she traveled and went about her outdoor work.

Infant girls were killed more often than boys for two reasons. First, in Eskimo society, the primary food providers were males—men were the hunters. Males were thus highly valued, because food was scarce. Second, the hunters suffered a high casualty rate. Eskimo men thus died prematurely far more often than Eskimo women did. If male and female infants had survived in equal numbers, then the female adult population would have greatly outnumbered the male adult population. Examining the available statistics, one writer concluded that "were it not for female infanticide . . . there would be approximately one-and-a-half times as many females in the average Eskimo local group as there are food-producing males."

Thus, Eskimo infanticide was not due to a fundamental disregard for children. Instead, it arose from the fact that drastic measures were needed to ensure the group's survival. And even then, killing the baby was always seen as the last resort—adoptions were common. Hence, Eskimo values were much like our own. It is only that life forced choices upon them that we do not have to make.

2.6. Some Values Are Shared by All Cultures

It should not surprise us that the Eskimos were protective of their children. How could they not have been? Babies are helpless and cannot survive without extensive care. If a group did not protect its young, the young would not survive, and the older members of the group would not be replaced. Eventually, the group would die out. This means that any enduring culture must have a tradition of caring for its children. Neglected infants must be the exception, not the rule.

Similar reasoning shows why honesty must be valued in every culture. Imagine what it would be like for a society to place no value on truth telling. In such a place, when one person spoke to another, there would be no presumption that she was being honest; she could just as easily be lying. Within that society, there would be no reason to pay attention to what anyone says. If, for example, I want to know what time it is, why should I bother asking anyone, if lying is commonplace? Communication would be extremely difficult, if not impossible, in such a society. And because societies cannot exist without communication among their members, society would become impossible. It follows that every society must value truthfulness. There may, of course, be situations in which lying is permitted, but the society will still value honesty in most situations.

Consider another example. Could a society exist in which there was no rule against murder? What would such a place be like? Suppose people were free to kill one another at will, and no one disapproved. In such a society, no one could feel safe. Everyone would have to be constantly on guard, and everyone would try to avoid other people—those potential murderers—as much as possible. This would result in individuals trying to become self-sufficient. Society on any large scale would thus be impossible. Of course, people might still band together in smaller groups where they could feel safe. But notice what this means: They would be forming smaller societies that did acknowledge a rule against murder. The prohibition against murder, then, is a necessary feature of society.

There is a general point here, namely, that *there are some moral rules that all societies must embrace, because those rules are necessary for society to exist.* The rules against lying and murder are two examples. And, in fact, we do find these rules in force in all cultures. Cultures may differ in what they regard as legitimate exceptions to the rules, but the rules themselves are the same. Therefore, we shouldn't overestimate the extent to which cultures differ. Not every moral rule can vary from society to society.

A further point is that societies will often have the same values due to their shared human nature. There are some things that, in every society, most people want. For example, people everywhere want clean water, leisure time, good health care, and the freedom to choose their own friends. Common goals will often yield common values.

2.7. Judging a Cultural Practice to Be Undesirable

In 1996, a 17-year-old named Fauziya Kassindja arrived at Newark International Airport in New Jersey and asked for asylum. She had fled her native country of Togo, in West Africa, to escape what people there call "excision." Excision is a permanently disfiguring procedure. It is sometimes called "female circumcision," but it bears little resemblance to male circumcision. In the West, it is usually referred to as "female genital mutilation."

According to the World Health Organization, more than 200 million living females have been excised. The cutting has occurred in 30 countries across Africa, the Middle East, and Asia. Sometimes excision is part of an elaborate tribal ritual performed in small villages, and girls look forward to it as their entry into the adult world. Other times, it is carried out in cities on young women who desperately resist.

Fauziya Kassindja was the youngest of five daughters. Her father, who owned a successful trucking business, was opposed to excision, and he was able to defy the tradition because of his wealth. Hence, his first four daughters were married without being mutilated. But when Fauziya was 16, he suddenly died. She then came under the authority of her aunt, who arranged a marriage for her and prepared to have her excised. Fauziya was terrified, and other members of her family helped her escape.

In America, Fauziya was imprisoned for nearly 18 months while the authorities decided what to do with her. During this time, she was subjected to humiliating strip searches, denied medical treatment for her asthma, and generally treated like a criminal. Finally, she was granted asylum, but not before her case aroused a great controversy. The controversy was not about her treatment in America, but about how we should regard the customs of other cultures. A series of articles in *The New York Times* encouraged the idea that excision is barbaric and should be condemned. Other observers, however, were reluctant to be so judgmental. Live and let live, they said; after all, our culture probably seems just as strange to the Africans.

Suppose we say that excision is wrong. Are we merely imposing the standards of our own culture? If Cultural Relativism is correct, that is all we can do, for there are no culture-independent moral standards. But is that true?

Is There a Culture-Independent Standard of Right and Wrong?
Excision is bad in many ways. It is painful and results in the permanent loss of sexual pleasure. Its short-term effects can include severe bleeding, problems urinating, and septicemia. Sometimes it causes death. Its long-term effects can include chronic infection, cysts, and scars that hinder walking.

Why, then, has it become a widespread social practice? It is not easy to say. Excision has no obvious social benefits. Unlike Eskimo infanticide, it is not necessary for group survival. Nor is it a matter of religion. Excision is practiced by groups from various religions, including Islam and Christianity.

Nevertheless, a number of arguments are made in its defense. Women who are incapable of sexual pleasure are less likely to be promiscuous; so, there will be fewer unwanted pregnancies in unmarried women. Moreover, wives for whom sex is only a duty are less likely to cheat on their husbands; and because they are not thinking about sex, they will be more attentive to the needs of their husbands and children. Husbands, for their part, are said to enjoy sex more with wives who have been excised. Unexcised women, the husbands feel, are unclean and immature.

It would be easy to ridicule these arguments; they are flawed in many respects. But notice an important feature of them: They try to justify excision by showing that excision is beneficial—men, women, and their families are said to be better off when women are excised. Thus, we might approach the issue by asking whether excision, on the whole, is helpful or harmful.

This points to a standard that might reasonably be used in thinking about any social practice: *Does the practice promote or hinder the welfare of the people affected by it?* This standard may be used to assess the practices of any culture at any time. Of course, people will not usually see it as being "brought in from the outside" to judge them, because all cultures value human happiness. Nevertheless, this looks like just the sort of culture-independent moral standard that Cultural Relativism forbids.

Why, Despite All This, Thoughtful People May Be Reluctant to Criticize Other Cultures. Many people who are horrified by excision are nevertheless reluctant to condemn it, for three reasons. First, there is an understandable nervousness about interfering in the social customs of other peoples. Europeans and their descendants in America have a shameful history of destroying native cultures in the name of Christianity and enlightenment. Because of this, some people refuse to criticize other cultures, especially cultures that resemble those that were wronged in the past.

However, there is a big difference between (a) judging a cultural practice to be deficient and (b) thinking that our leaders should announce that fact, apply diplomatic pressure, and send in the troops. The first is just a matter of trying to see the world clearly, from a moral point of view. The second is something else entirely. Sometimes it may be right to "do something about it," but often it will not be.

Second, people may feel, rightly enough, that we should be tolerant of other cultures. Tolerance, no doubt, is a virtue; a tolerant person can live in peace with those who see things differently. But nothing about tolerance requires us to say that all beliefs, all religions, and all social practices are equally admirable. On the contrary, if we did not view some things as better than others, then we would have nothing to tolerate.

Finally, people may be reluctant to judge because they do not want to express contempt for the society being criticized. But, again, this is misguided: To condemn a particular custom is not to condemn an entire culture. After all, a culture with a flaw can still have many admirable features. Indeed, we should expect this to be true of all human societies—all human societies are mixtures of good and bad practices. Excision happens to be one of the bad ones.

2.8. Back to the Five Claims

Let us now return to the five tenets of Cultural Relativism listed earlier. How have they fared in our discussion?

1. Different societies have different moral codes.

This is certainly true, although some values are shared by all cultures, such as the value of truth telling, the importance of caring for the young, and the prohibition against murder. Also, when customs differ, the underlying reason will often have more to do with the factual beliefs of the cultures than with their values.

2. The moral code of a society determines what is right within that society; so, if a society says that a certain action is right, then that action *is* right, at least in that society.

Here we must bear in mind the difference between what a society *believes* about morals and what is *really true*. The moral code of a society is closely tied to what people in that society believe about morals. However, those people, and that code, can be wrong. Earlier, we considered the example of excision—a barbaric practice endorsed by many societies. Consider two more examples, involving the mistreatment of women:

- In 2002, an unmarried mother in Nigeria was sentenced to be stoned to death for having had sex outside of marriage. It is unclear whether Nigerian values, on the whole, approved of this verdict, given that it was later overturned by a higher Nigerian court. However, it was overturned partly to please people outside of Nigeria—namely, the horrified international community. When the verdict was actually pronounced, the Nigerians who were there cheered and celebrated.
- In 2007, a woman was gang-raped in Saudi Arabia. When she went to the police, the police arrested *her* for having

been alone with a man she was not related to. For that crime, she was sentenced to 90 lashes. When she appealed her conviction, the judges increased her sentence to 200 lashes plus a six-month prison term. Eventually, the Saudi king pardoned her, while also saying that the judges had given her the right sentence.

Cultural Relativism holds, in effect, that societies are morally infallible—in other words, that the morals of a culture can never be wrong. But when we see that societies can and do endorse grave injustices, we see that societies, like their members, can be in need of moral improvement.

3. There is no objective standard that can be used to judge one society's code as better than another's. There are no moral truths that hold for all people at all times.

It is difficult to think of ethical principles that should hold for all people at all times. However, if we are to criticize the practice of slavery, or stoning, or genital mutilation, and if such practices are really and truly wrong, then we must appeal to principles that are not tethered to the traditions of any particular society. Earlier I suggested one such principle: that it always matters whether a practice helps or hurts the people who are affected by it.

4. The moral code of our own society has no special status; it is but one among many.

It is true that the moral code of our society has no special status. After all, our society has no heavenly halo around its borders; our values do not have any special standing just because they happen to be endorsed in the place where we grew up. However, to say that the moral code of one's own society "is merely one among many" seems to imply that all codes are the same—that they are all more or less equally good. In fact, it is an open question whether the code of one's society "is merely one among many." That code might be among the best; it might be among the worst.

5. It is arrogant for us to judge other cultures. We should always be tolerant of them.

There is much truth in this, but the point is overstated. We *are* often arrogant when we criticize other cultures, and tolerance *is* generally a good thing. However, we shouldn't tolerate everything. The toleration of torture, slavery, and rape is a vice, not a virtue.

2.9. What We Can Learn from Cultural Relativism

So far, in discussing Cultural Relativism, I have dwelt mostly on its shortcomings. I have said that it rests on an unsound argument, that it has implausible consequences, and that it exaggerates how much moral disagreement there is between societies. This all adds up to a rejection of the theory. Nevertheless, you may feel like this is a little unfair. The theory must have something going for it—why else has it been so influential? In fact, I think there is something right about Cultural Relativism, and there are two lessons we should learn from it.

First, Cultural Relativism warns us, quite rightly, about the danger of assuming that all of our practices are based on some absolute rational standard. They are not. Some of our customs are merely conventional—merely peculiar to how we do things—and it is easy to forget that. In reminding us of this, the theory does us a service.

Funeral practices are one example. The Callatians, according to Herodotus, were "men who eat their fathers"—a shocking idea, to us at least. But eating the flesh of the dead could be understood as a sign of respect. It could be seen as a symbolic act that says, "This person's spirit shall dwell inside us." Perhaps this is how the Callatians saw it. On this way of thinking, burying the dead could be seen as an act of rejection, and burning the dead could be seen as being positively scornful. Of course, the idea of eating human flesh may repel us, but so what? Our revulsion may only be a reflection of where we were raised. Cultural Relativism begins with the insight that many of our practices are like this—they are only cultural products. Then it goes wrong by assuming that all of them are.

Or consider a more complex example: monogamous marriage. In our society, the ideal is to fall in love, get married, and remain faithful to that one person forever. But aren't there other ways to pursue happiness? The writer Dan Savage lists some possible drawbacks of monogamy: "boredom, despair, lack of variety, sexual death and being taken for granted." For such reasons, many people regard monogamy as an unrealistic goal—and as a goal whose pursuit would not make them happy.

What are the alternatives to this ideal? Some married couples reject monogamy by giving each other permission to have the occasional extramarital fling. Allowing one's spouse to have an affair is risky—one might feel too jealous, or the spouse might not come back—but greater openness in marriage might work better than our current system, in which many people feel ashamed, sexually trapped, and unable to discuss their feelings. Other people deviate from monogamy more radically by having more than one long-term partner, with the consent of everyone involved. In these "open" relationships, the emphasis is on honesty and transparency rather than fidelity. Some of these arrangements might work better than others, but this is not really a matter of morality. If a man's wife gives him permission to have sex with another woman, then he isn't "cheating" on her—he isn't betraying her trust, because she consented to the affair. Or, if four people want to live together and function as a single family, with love flowing from each to each, then there is nothing morally wrong with that. Yet most people in our society would disapprove of any deviation from monogamy.

The second lesson has to do with keeping an open mind. As we grow up, we develop strong feelings about things: We learn to see some types of behavior as acceptable, and other types as outrageous. Occasionally we may find our feelings challenged. For example, we may have been taught that homosexuality is immoral, and we may feel uncomfortable around gay people. But then someone suggests that our feelings are unjustified; that there is nothing wrong with being gay; and that gay people are just people, like anyone else, who happen to be attracted to members of the same sex. Because we feel so strongly about this, we may find it hard to take seriously the idea that we are prejudiced.

Cultural Relativism provides an antidote for this kind of dogmatism. When he tells the story of the Greeks and Callatians, Herodotus adds,

> For if anyone, no matter who, were given the opportunity of choosing from amongst all the nations of the world the set of beliefs which he thought best, he would inevitably, after careful consideration of their relative merits, choose that of his own country. Everyone without exception believes his own native customs, and the religion he was brought up in, to be the best.

Realizing this can help broaden our minds. We can see that our feelings are not necessarily perceptions of the truth; they may be due to cultural conditioning and nothing more. Thus, when we hear a criticism of our culture, and we find ourselves becoming angry and defensive, we might stop and remember this. Then we will be more open to discovering the truth, whatever it might be.

We can understand the appeal of Cultural Relativism, then, despite its shortcomings. It is an attractive theory because it is based on a genuine insight: that many of the practices and attitudes we find natural are only cultural products. Moreover, keeping this thought in mind is important if we want to avoid arrogance and be open to new ideas. These are important points, not to be taken lightly. But we can accept them without accepting the whole theory.

Notes on Sources

The story of the Greeks and the Callatians is from Herodotus, *The Histories*, translated by Aubrey de Selincourt, revised by A. R. Burn (Harmondsworth, Middlesex: Penguin Books, 1972), pp. 219–220. The quotation from Herodotus toward the end of the chapter is from the same source.

The information about the Eskimos is from Peter Freuchen, *Book of the Eskimos* (New York: Fawcett, 1961), and E. Adamson Hoebel, *The Law of Primitive Man* (Cambridge, MA: Harvard University Press, 1954), chapter 5. The estimate of how female infanticide affects the male/female ratio in the Eskimo population is from Hoebel.

William Graham Sumner, *Folkways* (Boston: Ginn, 1906), p. 28.

The New York Times series on female genital mutilation included articles (mainly by Celia W. Dugger) published in 1996 on April 15, April 25, May 2, May 3, July 8, September 11, October 5, October 12, and December 28. I learned much about Fauziya Kassindja from her PBS interview; see http://www.pbs.org/speaktruthtopower/fauziya.html. The figures from the World Health Organization are from the WHO's fact sheet on "Female Genital Mutilation" (updated February 2017), at http://www.who.int/mediacentre/factsheets/fs241/en/.

The story about the Nigerian woman sentenced to death is from Associated Press articles on August 20, 2002, and September 25, 2003. The story about the Saudi woman who was sentenced to being lashed comes from *The New York Times* (articles on November 16 and December 18, 2007).

Dan Savage is quoted by Mark Oppenheimer, "Married, with Infidelities," *The New York Times Magazine*, July 3, 2011, pp. 22–27, 46 (quotation on p. 23).

CHAPTER 3

Subjectivism in Ethics

Take any [vicious] action. . . . Willful murder, for instance. Examine it
in all lights, and see if you can find that matter of fact, or real existence,
which you call vice. . . . You can never find it, till you turn your
reflection into your own breast, and find a sentiment of [disapproval],
which arises in you, toward this action. Here is a matter of fact; but 'tis
the object of feeling, not reason.
DAVID HUME, *A TREATISE OF HUMAN NATURE* (1739-1740)

3.1. The Basic Idea of Ethical Subjectivism

In 2001 there was a mayoral election in New York, and when it
came time for the city's Gay Pride Day parade, every single
Democratic and Republican candidate showed up to march. Matt
Foreman, the director of a gay rights organization, described all the
candidates as "good on our issues." He said, "In other parts of the
country, the positions taken here would be extremely unpopular, if
not deadly, at the polls." The national Republican Party apparently
agrees; for decades, it has opposed the gay rights movement.

What do people around the country actually think? Since the
year of that parade, 2001, the Gallup Poll has been asking Americans
their personal opinions about gay and lesbian relations. In 2001,
only 40% of Americans considered gay relations to be "morally
acceptable," while 53% viewed them as "morally wrong." By 2017,
these numbers had changed dramatically: 63% saw gay relations as
"morally acceptable," whereas only 33% deemed them "morally
wrong."

People on both sides have strong feelings. As a member of
Congress, Mike Pence spoke out against gay marriage on the

floor of the House of Representatives. Calling traditional marriage "the backbone of our society," he warned America that "societal collapse" always follows "the deterioration of marriage and family."

Pence is an evangelical Christian. The Catholic view may be more nuanced, but it agrees that gay sex is wrong. According to the *Catechism of the Catholic Church*, gays "do not choose their homosexual condition" and "must be accepted with respect, compassion, and sensitivity. Every sign of unjust discrimination in their regard should be avoided." Nonetheless, "homosexual acts are intrinsically disordered" and "under no circumstances can they be approved." So, gay people must resist their desires if they want to be virtuous.

What attitude should we take? We might think that gay relations are immoral, or we might find them acceptable. But there is a third alternative. We might believe:

> People have different opinions, but where morality is concerned, there are no "facts," and no one is "right." People just feel differently about things, and that's all there is to it.

This is the basic idea behind Ethical Subjectivism. Ethical Subjectivism is the theory that our moral opinions are based on our feelings and nothing more. As David Hume (1711–1776) put it, morality is a matter of "sentiment" rather than "reason." According to this theory, there is no such thing as right or wrong. It is a fact that some people are gay and that some people are straight, but it is not a fact that being gay is morally better or morally worse than being straight.

Of course, Ethical Subjectivism is not merely an idea about same-sex relations. It applies to all moral matters. To take a different example, it is a fact that over half a million abortions are performed in the United States each year. However, according to Ethical Subjectivism, it is not a fact that this is morally acceptable or morally wrong. When pro-life activists call abortion "murder," they are merely expressing their outrage. And when pro-choice activists say that a woman should have the right to choose, they are merely letting us know how they feel.

3.2. The Linguistic Turn

What's startling about Ethical Subjectivism is its view of moral value. If ethics has no objective basis, then morality is all just opinion, and our sense that some things are "really" right or "really" wrong is just an illusion. However, most of the moral philosophers who developed this theory did not focus on its implications for value. Toward the end of the 19th century, professional philosophy took a "linguistic turn," as philosophers began to work almost exclusively on questions of language and meaning. This trend lasted until around 1970. During that time-period, Ethical Subjectivism was developed by philosophers who asked such questions as: What exactly do people mean when they use words like "good" and "bad"? What is the purpose of moral language? What are moral debates about, if they're not about whose opinion is (really) correct? With questions like those in mind, philosophers proposed various versions of the theory.

Simple Subjectivism. The simplest version is this: When a person says that something is morally good or bad, this means that he or she approves of that thing, or disapproves of it, and nothing more. In other words:

"X is morally acceptable"
"X is right"
"X is good"
"X ought to be done"
⎫
all mean: "I (the speaker) approve of X"

And similarly:

"X is morally unacceptable"
"X is wrong"
"X is bad"
"X ought not to be done"
⎫
all mean: "I (the speaker) disapprove of X"

Let's call this version of the theory *Simple Subjectivism*. It expresses the basic idea of Ethical Subjectivism in a plain, uncomplicated form. However, it is open to a serious objection.

The objection is that Simple Subjectivism cannot account for moral disagreement. Let's consider our previous example. Gay rights advocate Matt Foreman believes that being gay is morally acceptable. Mike Pence believes that it is not. So, Foreman and Pence disagree. But consider what Simple Subjectivism implies about this situation.

When Foreman says that being gay is morally acceptable, the theory says that he is merely saying something about his attitudes—he is saying, "I, Matt Foreman, do not disapprove of being gay." Would Pence disagree with that? No, he would agree that Foreman does not disapprove of being gay. At the same time, when Pence says that being gay is immoral, he is only saying, "I, Mike Pence, disapprove of being gay." And how could anyone doubt that? Thus, according to Simple Subjectivism, there is no disagreement between them; each should acknowledge the truth of what the other is saying. Surely, though, this is incorrect, because Pence and Foreman *do* disagree.

There is a kind of eternal frustration implied by Simple Subjectivism: Pence and Foreman have deeply opposing points of view, yet they cannot state their beliefs in a way that manifests their disagreement. Foreman may try to deny what Pence says, but, according to Simple Subjectivism, he succeeds only in talking about himself.

The argument may be summarized like this: When one person says, "X is morally acceptable," and someone else says, "X is morally unacceptable," they are disagreeing. However, if Simple Subjectivism were correct, then they would not be. Therefore, Simple Subjectivism cannot be correct. This argument seems to show that Simple Subjectivism is flawed.

Emotivism. The next version of Ethical Subjectivism came to be known as *Emotivism*. Emotivism was popular during the mid-20th century, largely due to the American philosopher Charles L. Stevenson (1908–1979).

Language, Stevenson observed, is used in many ways. Sometimes it is used to make statements—that is, to state facts. Thus we may say,

"Gas prices are rising."

"Quarterback Peyton Manning underwent multiple neck surgeries, was sidelined for a year, and then broke the record for most touchdown passes in a season."

"Shakespeare wrote *Hamlet*."

In each case, we are saying something that is either true or false, and the purpose of our utterance is, typically, to convey information to our audience.

However, language is also used for other purposes. Suppose I say, "Close the door!" This utterance is neither true nor false. It is not a statement, intended to convey information; it is a command. Its purpose is to get someone to do something.

Or consider utterances such as these, which are neither statements nor commands:

"Aaargh!"

"Way to go, Peyton!"

"Alas, poor Yorick!"

We understand these sentences easily enough. But none of them can be true or false. (It makes no sense to say, "It is true that 'way to go, Peyton'" or "It is false that 'aaargh.'") These sentences are not used to state facts or to influence behavior. Their purpose is to express the speaker's attitudes—attitudes about gas prices, or Peyton Manning, or Yorick.

Now think about moral language. According to Simple Subjectivism, moral language is about stating facts—ethical judgments are reports of the speaker's attitudes. According to that theory, when Pence says, "Being gay is immoral," his utterance means "I (Pence) disapprove of being gay"—a statement of fact about Pence's attitudes. However, according to Emotivism, moral language is not fact-stating; it is not used to convey information. It is used, first, as a means of influencing people's behavior. If someone says, "You shouldn't do that," he is trying to *persuade you not to do it*; his utterance is more like a command than a statement of fact. "You shouldn't do that" is a gentler way of saying, "Don't do that!" Second, moral language is used to express attitudes. Calling Peyton Manning "a morally good man" is like saying, "Way to go, Peyton!" And so, when Pence says, "Being gay is immoral," emotivists interpret his utterance as meaning something like "Homosexuality—gross!" or "Don't be gay!"

Earlier we saw that Simple Subjectivism cannot account for moral disagreement. Can Emotivism?

According to Emotivism, disagreement comes in different forms. Compare these two ways in which people can clash:

• I believe that Lee Harvey Oswald acted alone in killing President John F. Kennedy, and you believe that Oswald was

part of a conspiracy. This is a factual disagreement—I believe something to be true which you believe to be false.
- I am rooting for the Atlanta Braves baseball team to win, and you are rooting for them to lose. Our beliefs are not in conflict, but our desires are—I want something to happen which you want not to happen.

In the first case, we believe different things, both of which cannot be true. Stevenson calls this *disagreement in belief*. In the second case, we want different outcomes, both of which cannot occur. Stevenson calls this *disagreement in attitude*. Our attitudes may be different even when our beliefs aren't. For example, you and I may have all the same beliefs regarding the Atlanta Braves: We both believe that Braves players are overpaid; we both believe that I am rooting for the Braves just because I am from the South; and we both believe that Atlanta is not a great baseball town. Yet despite all this common ground—despite all this agreement *in belief*—we may still disagree *in attitude*: I may still root for the Braves, and you may still root against them.

According to Stevenson, moral disagreement is disagreement in attitude. Matt Foreman and Mike Pence may (or may not) have clashing beliefs about the facts regarding homosexuality. Yet it is clear that they disagree in attitude. For example, Foreman wants same-sex marriage to remain legal in the United States, whereas Pence does not. For Emotivism, then, moral conflict is real.

Is Emotivism correct? It has the virtue of identifying some of the main functions of moral language. Certainly, moral language is used to persuade and to express our attitudes. However, in denying that moral language is fact-stating, Emotivism seems to be denying an obvious truth. For example, when I say, "Long-term solitary confinement is a cruel punishment," it is true that I disapprove of such punishment, and it may also be true that I am trying to persuade someone else to oppose it. However, I am also trying to say something that is true; I am making a statement that I believe to be correct. Like most people, I do not see my own moral convictions as "mere opinions" that are no more justified than the beliefs of bigots, bullies, and bumbling fools. The fact that I see things in this way, whether rightly or wrongly, is relevant to interpreting what I mean when I use words like "ought," "good," and "wrong."

The Error Theory. The last version of Ethical Subjectivism acknowl-edges that people are at least *trying* to say true things when they talk about ethics. This is the *Error Theory* of John L. Mackie (1917–1981). Mackie was a subjectivist; he believed that there are no "facts" in ethics, and that no one is ever "right" or "wrong." However, he also saw that people *believe* they are right, and so we should interpret them as *trying* to state objective truths. Thus, instead of saying that Pence and Foreman are merely reporting their own attitudes (Simple Subjectivism) or expressing their own feelings (Emotivism), the Error Theory holds that Pence and Foreman are in error: they are each making a positive claim about value—in claiming that the moral truth is on their side—even though no such truth exists. Moral discussions, Mackie thought, are teeming with error.

3.3. The Denial of Value

Moral theories are primarily about value, not language. Hence, our discussion of Ethical Subjectivism might seem to have gone off track. At the heart of Ethical Subjectivism is a theory of value called *Nihilism*. Nihilists believe that values are not real. People might have various moral beliefs, but, really, nothing is good or bad, or right or wrong. Earlier we applied Nihilism to the issues of abortion and same-sex relations. According to a nihilist, neither side is right in those debates, because there is no "right."

So long as we consider only difficult or controversial moral issues, Nihilism might seem plausible. After all, we may ourselves be unsure what to think about such issues; perhaps we're unsure because there's no right answer? Yet Nihilism and Ethical Subjectivism seem much less plausible when applied to simpler matters. To take a new example: It is a fact that the Nazis killed millions of people based on their racial backgrounds, but, according to Nihilism, it is not a fact that the Nazis acted badly. Instead, the nihilist would say that different people have different opinions, and no one is right. You may believe one thing, but Adolph Hitler believes something else, and Hitler's opinion is just as good as yours.

Viewed in this light, Nihilism seems absurd. Indeed, it is hard to believe that anyone has ever believed Nihilism, or at least believed it consistently. After all, every human being has moral beliefs in addition to having "subjective feelings." Even racists believe that it would be wrong to kill *them* or to exterminate *their race*; yet those judgments also conflict with Subjectivism.

Nihilism might be compared to another theory, which has nothing to do with ethics. According to this theory, the universe is only five minutes old. Such a theory denies the existence of the past—or, at least, of a past that stretches back more than five minutes. This theory, although ridiculous, is hard to refute. If you try to refute it by describing events that you recall happening yesterday, the reply will be that your "memories" of those events were put in your brain five minutes ago, when the universe came into being. Or, if you point to a book with a copyright date of 1740, the reply will be that this book came into existence—along with its misleading copyright page—exactly five minutes ago.

Such a position is hard to refute, but none of us are tempted to believe it. Much the same can be said about Nihilism and Ethical Subjectivism. These theories deny the existence of right and wrong. So, for example, they deny that it is wrong to intentionally cause severe pain to a human baby for no reason. A nihilist would simply say that the baby-torturer has *his* beliefs on the matter, and that you and I have ours. Such a position may be hard to refute, but perhaps a refutation isn't necessary.

3.4. Ethics and Science

If Ethical Subjectivism is so implausible, then why are so many people attracted to it? Perhaps some people haven't considered its implications very carefully. Yet there are deeper reasons for its appeal. Many thoughtful people feel they must be skeptical about values, if they are to maintain a proper respect for science.

According to one line of thought, a belief in "objective values" in the 21st century is like a belief in ghosts or witches or mystics. If there are such things, then why hasn't science discovered them? Even back in the 18th century, David Hume argued that if we examine wicked actions—"willful murder, for instance"—we will find no "real existence" corresponding to the wickedness. The universe contains no such thing as wickedness; our belief in it comes merely from our subjective responses. As Mackie put it, values are not part of "the fabric of the world."

What should we make of this? Admittedly, value is not a tangible thing like a planet or a spoon. Scientists will never "discover" wickedness, as they might discover a new type of electron. However, this does not mean that ethics has no objective basis. A common mistake is to assume that there are just two possibilities:

1. There are moral values, in the same way that there are planets and spoons.
2. Our values are nothing more than the expression of our subjective feelings.

This overlooks a third possibility. People have not only feelings but reason, and that makes a big difference. It may be that

3. Moral truths are matters of reason; a moral judgment is true if it is backed by better reasons than the alternatives.

On this view, moral truths are objective in the sense that they are true independently of what we might want or believe. If there are good reasons against inflicting pain on babies, and no good reasons on the other side, then it is objectively true—and not "mere opinion"—that causing such pain is wrong.

Another line of thought takes science as our model of objectivity. But when we compare ethics to science, ethics seems lacking. For example, there are proofs in science, but there are no proofs in ethics. We can prove that the earth is round, that dinosaurs lived before humans, and that bodies are made up of atoms. But we can't prove whether abortion is acceptable or unacceptable.

The idea that moral judgments can't be proved seems appealing. However, as we noted earlier, the subjectivist's case seems strongest when we consider difficult issues like abortion. When we think about such matters, it is easy to believe that "proof" is impossible. Yet there are also complicated matters in science that scientists argue about. If we focused entirely on those issues, we might conclude that there are no proofs in physics or chemistry or biology.

Suppose we consider a simpler moral matter. A student says that a test was unfair. This is clearly a moral judgment; fairness is a moral idea. Can this judgment be proved? The student might point out that the test covered a lot of trivial material while ignoring what the teacher had stressed. The test also covered material that was neither in the readings nor in class discussions. Moreover, the test was so long that nobody could finish it.

Suppose all this is true. Further suppose that the teacher has no defense to offer. In fact, the teacher, who is new to teaching, seems generally confused. Hasn't the student *proved* that the test was unfair? It is easy to think of other examples that make the same point:

- *Jones is a bad man:* Jones is a habitual liar; he enjoys ridiculing people; he cheats at cards; he once killed a man in a dispute over 27 cents; and so on.
- *Dr. Smith is irresponsible:* She bases her diagnoses on superficial considerations; she doesn't listen to other doctors' advice; she drinks cheap American beer before performing delicate surgery; and so on.
- *Joe the used-car dealer is immoral:* He conceals defects in his cars; he tries to pressure people into paying too much; he runs misleading ads on the Web; and so on.

The process of giving reasons can be taken further. If we criticize Jones for being a habitual liar, we can go on to explain why lying is bad. Lying is bad, first, because it harms people. If I give you false information, and you rely on it, things may go wrong for you in all sorts of ways. Second, lying is a violation of trust. Trusting another person means leaving yourself vulnerable and unprotected. When I trust you, I simply believe what you say, without taking precautions; and when you lie, you take advantage of my trust. Finally, the rule requiring truthfulness is necessary for society to exist. If we could not trust what other people said, then communication would be impossible. If communication were impossible, then society would fall apart.

So we can support our judgments with good reasons, and we can explain why those reasons matter. If we can do all this and, for an encore, show that no comparable case can be made on the other side, what more in the way of "proof" could anyone want? Perhaps people want ethical theories to be proved experimentally, the way scientific theories are. However, in ethics, proving a hypothesis involves giving reasons, analyzing arguments, setting out and justifying principles, and so on. The fact that ethical reasoning differs from scientific reasoning does not mean that ethics is deficient.

Despite all this, anyone who has ever argued about something like abortion knows how frustrating it can be to try to "prove" one's opinion. Yet we must not run together two things that are really very different:

1. Proving an opinion to be correct
2. Persuading someone to accept your proof

Constructing sound proofs is part of philosophy. However, philosophers leave persuasion to the psychologists, politicians, and product advertisers. From a philosophical perspective, an argument may be a good proof even if it fails as persuasion. After all, an argument may be unpersuasive merely because those who hear it are stubborn or biased or not really listening.

3.5. Same-Sex Relations

Let's return to the dispute about gays. If we consider the relevant reasons, what do we find? The most pertinent fact is that gays are pursuing the only kind of life that can make them happy. Sex, after all, is a particularly strong urge, and few people can be happy without satisfying their sexual needs. But we should not focus solely on sex. Being gay is not merely about sex; it's also about love. Gay people develop crushes and fall in love in the same way that straight people do. And, like straight people, gay people often want to live with, and be with, the person they love. To say that homosexuals shouldn't act on their desires is thus to wish unhappiness on those human beings. Nor can we pretend that they might avoid loneliness and frustration by choosing to become straight. Both homosexuals and heterosexuals discover who they are, once they reach a certain age; nobody decides which sex to be attracted to.

Arguments against Homosexuality. Why do people oppose gay rights? Some folks think homosexuals are "dangerous perverts." The charge, often merely insinuated, is that gay men are especially likely to molest children. In the mid-to-late 20th century, there were several campaigns in America to get gay schoolteachers fired, and those campaigns always played on the fears of parents. Before serving in Congress, Michele Bachmann exploited this fear in 2004 when she said that gay marriage "is a very serious matter, because it is our children who are the prize for [the gay] community—they are specifically targeting our children." Such a fear, however, has never been justified. It is a mere stereotype, like the idea that Muslims are terrorists or that black people are lazy. Gay people are not more likely to molest children than straight people.

A different argument faults homosexuality for being "unnatural." What should we make of this charge? To assess it, we must understand it. In particular, we need to understand what "unnatural" means. There seem to be three possibilities.

First, "unnatural" might merely be a statistical idea. A human quality is unnatural, in this sense, if few people possess it. Being gay would be unnatural—because most people aren't gay—but so would being left-handed, being tall, and even being especially nice or especially courageous. Clearly, the statistical notion gives us no reason to condemn homosexuality. Many rare qualities are good.

Second, "unnatural" might be connected to a thing's *purpose.* Parts of the human body seem to serve specific purposes, and it seems wrong when they don't or won't. Fingers that cannot bend in order to grasp objects are *arthritic*; kidneys that cannot remove toxins are *diseased.* And so, the argument goes, the genitals serve the purpose of procreation; sex is for making babies. Thus, gay sex is *unnatural* because it involves using the genitals in ways that cannot produce children.

This idea seems to express what many people mean when they say that homosexuality is unnatural. Yet to condemn gay sex on these grounds would also condemn several widely accepted practices that *heterosexuals* engage in: masturbation, oral sex, sex using birth control, online sex and virtual sex, sex had by pregnant women, and sex involving someone who is sterile, including men who have had vasectomies and women who have gone through menopause. None of these sexual activities can result in pregnancy; thus, all might be condemned as "unnatural." However, we needn't do that, because this whole way of reasoning is faulty. It rests on the assumption that *it is wrong to use one's body parts for anything other than their natural purposes.* And why should we believe that? The natural purpose of the eyes is to see; is it, therefore, wrong to use one's eyes to flirt or to express surprise? The fingers are meant to grasp and poke; is it, therefore, wrong to snap one's fingers in order to get someone's attention? Why can't we invent new purposes for things? The idea that things should be used only in "natural" ways cannot be maintained, and so the second version of the argument also fails.

Third, because the word "unnatural" has a sinister sound, it might be understood simply as a term of evaluation. Perhaps it means something like "contrary to how things ought to be." But then to say that homosexuality is wrong because it is *unnatural* is to say that homosexuality is wrong because it is contrary to how things ought to be—which is a lot like saying that it's wrong because it's wrong. That sort of empty remark provides no reason to condemn anything.

Hence, no meaning for "unnatural" yields a sound argument. Homosexual behavior doesn't seem to be unnatural in any troubling sense.

Finally, let's consider the argument that homosexuality is wrong because the Bible condemns it. For example, Leviticus 18:22 says, "You may not lie with a man as with a woman; it is an abomination." And suppose we agree that the Bible really does condemn homosexuality. What may we infer from this? Are we supposed to believe what the Bible says, simply because it says it?

This question will offend some people. To question the Bible, they believe, is to challenge the word of God. And this, they think, is an act of arrogance coming from creatures who should be thanking the Almighty for what they have. Questioning the Bible can also make people feel uncomfortable, because it may seem to challenge their whole way of life. However, thoughts like these cannot hold us back. Philosophy is about questioning ways of life. When the argument is given that homosexuality must be wrong because the Bible says so, the argument must be assessed on its merits, just like any other argument.

The problem with the argument is that, if we look at *other* things the Bible says, then it does not appear to be a reliable guide to morality. The Book of Leviticus condemns homosexuality, but it also forbids eating sheep's fat (7:23), letting a woman into the church's sanctuary who has recently given birth (12:2–5), and seeing your uncle naked. Seeing your uncle naked, like homosexuality, is considered an abomination (18:14, 26). Even worse, Leviticus condemns to death those who curse their parents (20:9) and those who commit adultery (20:10). It says that a priest's daughter, if she "plays the whore," shall be burned alive (21:9), and it says that we may purchase slaves from nearby nations (25:44). In Exodus, it even says that it's okay to beat your slaves, so long as you don't kill them (21:20–21).

The point of all this is not to ridicule the Bible; the Bible, in fact, contains much that is true and wise. But we can conclude from examples like these that the Bible is not always right. And because it's not always right, we can't conclude that homosexuality is an abomination just because the Bible says that it is.

Marriage, Adoption, and Not Getting Fired. In American politics, conservatives have often claimed that gay rights are "contrary to family values." When Mike Pence called traditional marriage "the glue of the American family," he was suggesting that the American family would fall apart if gay couples were allowed to marry. But why should it? Gays have never tried to change traditional families. Instead, they have tried to form their own families. They have sought the right to marry and the right to adopt children.

In 2015, the U.S. Supreme Court ruled that same-sex marriage is a right guaranteed by the U.S. Constitution. Hence, gay marriage is now legal in all fifty states. Adoption rights, however, are not yet guaranteed. Some states have "religious freedom laws" that allow private adoption agencies to turn away same-sex couples, if the people in those agencies believe that their religion forbids them from helping gay people become parents.

Personal beliefs aside, why shouldn't gay couples be allowed to raise children? For decades, the U.S. National Longitudinal Lesbian Family Study has followed a group of children who were born between 1986 and 1992 and raised by two mothers. At age 17, those children seemed to be doing *significantly better* than their peers who grew up in traditional homes. Sometimes, the teens were made fun of at school, and that was hard on them. But, in general, they were doing better than other teenagers, both socially and academically, and had fewer behavioral problems. Bear in mind, too, that the children in this study were 17 between 2003 and 2009. Since then, non-traditional families have become more common, and so today's teenager might also get teased less at school for having two moms. At any rate, the American Academy of Pediatrics supports full adoption rights for same-sex couples.

Gay people are also seeking legal protection at work. Anyone working in the United States for an employer who has 15 or more employees cannot be fired on the basis of sex, race, color, national origin, or religion; this is due to Title VII of the 1964 Civil Rights Act. Yet no federal law forbids firing someone on the basis of sexual orientation. Instead, the laws differ from state to state. In 28 states, it is legal to fire someone for being gay. In those states, it is also legal to fire someone for being straight, but that never happens.

Laws Abroad and Social Realities at Home. American law no longer discriminates blatantly against gays. However, many other countries' laws do. In 72 countries, gay sex is illegal. In eight places, homosexuality is punishable by death.

One intolerant place is Russia. Its "gay propaganda laws" forbid Russians from even *speaking* about homosexuality in public. Vladimir Putin, Russia's dictator, often criticizes the West for its "decadence," and his main example is always the toleration of gays. Police in the Russian republic of Chechnya combated such decadence in 2017 by rounding up and torturing at least 100 gay men, ultimately murdering at least three. The torture was used as a way of forcing the victim to lure other gay men into meeting him somewhere, thus giving the police a new victim to brutalize.

In America, the drawbacks to being gay are social rather than legal but can be serious. *How* serious may depend on where you live, and on who you interact with. But, in general, if you are gay, then you can expect that about one-third of your neighbors believe that something is wrong with you. And that can be stressful. Someone who is LGBT (lesbian, gay, bisexual, or transgender) runs a higher risk of being targeted in a hate crime than does a member of any other minority—including Jews and African-American. This was the case even before the massacre in Orlando in 2016, in which a single gunman murdered 49 people in a gay nightclub. In the aftermath of that slaughter, as emergency personnel tended to the horrific scene, they could hear the haunting, discordant sound of cell phones ringing in the pockets of the deceased, as their friends and loved ones called to see if they were okay.

Many gay people in the United States choose to live in the closet—some due to fear, some due to shame. But trying to hide who you are is always stressful. A common tragedy is when a young person who has been taught to despise gays begins to realize that he or she *is* gay. Young LGBTs are almost six times more likely than their peers to have recently attempted suicide—or, at least, that was true as of 2015. The good news is that society is becoming more tolerant, and so gay life is becoming more tolerable. The suicide rate for gay teens quickly fell by an average of 14% in particular individual states, once those states began recognizing the right of same-sex couples to say "I do."

Notes on Sources

Matt Foreman was quoted in *The New York Times* on June 25, 2001.

The Gallup Poll information is from www.gallup.com.

Mike Pence on marriage: see the *United States of America Congressional Record: Proceedings and Debates of the 109th Congress*, Second Session, Vol. 152, Part 11, p. 14,796 (pertaining to July 18, 2006).

The Catholic view of homosexuality is from *Catechism of the Catholic Church* (Mahwah, NJ: Paulist Press, 1994), p. 566.

Over half a million abortions performed per year: for example, in 2013, there were more than 664,000 abortions, according to cdc.gov.

Charles L. Stevenson on "disagreement in belief" and "disagreement in attitude": *Ethics and Language* (New Haven, CT: Yale University Press, 1944), pp. 2–4.

"[T]he fabric of the world": J. L. Mackie, *Ethics: Inventing Right and Wrong* (England: Penguin Books, 1977), p. 15.

Michele Bachmann was speaking on the radio program *Prophetic Views behind the News* (hosted by Jan Markell), KKMS 980-AM, March 20, 2004.

Gay people are not more likely to molest children: Olga Khazan, "Milo Yiannopoulos and the Myth of the Gay Pedophile," *The Atlantic*, February 21, 2017.

For state-by-state information on same-sex adoption laws, see "LGBT Adoption Laws" at lifelongadoptions.com.

Nanette Gartrell and Henny Bos, "U.S. National Longitudinal Lesbian Family Study: Psychological Adjustment of 17-Year-Old Adolescents," *Pediatrics* 126, no. 1 (July 2010), pp. 1–9.

See the American Academy of Pediatrics' Policy Statement, "Promoting the Well-Being of Children Whose Parents Are Gay or Lesbian," *Pediatrics*, vol. 131, no. 4 (April 1, 2013), pp. 827–830.

Gays can be fired in 28 states: see the "State Maps of Laws & Policies" on the Human Rights Campaign website (hrc.org).

Gay sex is illegal in 72 countries and is punishable by death in 8 (as of May 2017): International Lesbian, Gay, Bisexual, Trans and Intersex Association: Carroll, A., *State Sponsored Homophobia 2017: A World Survey of Sexual Orientation Laws: Criminalisation, Protection and Recognition* (Geneva; ILGA, May 2017), pp. 8, 9, and 37–38.

On Russia and Chechnya, see Sewell Chan, "Russia's 'Gay Propaganda' Laws Are Illegal, European Court Rules," *The New York Times*, June 20, 2017, and Andrew E. Kramer, "'They Starve You. They Shock You': Inside the Anti-Gay Pogrom in Chechnya," *The New York Times*, April 21, 2017.

On LGBT suicide attempts in 2015, see cdc.org, "Lesbian, Gay, Bisexual, and Transgender Health"/"LGBT Youth," accessed August 27, 2017. On hate crimes, see the FBI's 2015 Hate Crime Statistics (under "Victims") at ucr.fbi.gov (accessed August 27, 2017). Also see Haeyoun Park and Iaryna Mykhyalyshyn, "L.G.B.T. People Are More Likely to Be Targets of Hate Crimes Than Any Other Minority Group," *The New York Times*, June 16, 2016.

On suicide attempts by gay teens after 2015, see Julia Raifman et al., "Difference-in-Differences Analysis of the Association Between State Same-Sex Marriage Policies and Adolescent Suicide Attempts," *JAMA Pediatrics*, vol. 171, no. 4 (April 2017), pp. 350–356.

Christopher Bucktin, "Orlando Shooting Investigators Haunted by Sound of Mobile Phones as Families Try to Ring Victims," *Mirror*, June 12, 2016.

CHAPTER 4

Does Morality Depend on Religion?

The Good consists in always doing what God wills at any particular
moment.

EMIL BRUNNER, *THE DIVINE IMPERATIVE* (1947)

I respect deities. I do not rely upon them.

MUSASHI MIYAMOTO, AT ICHIJOJI TEMPLE (ca. 1608)

4.1. The Presumed Connection between Morality and Religion

In 1995, the American Civil Liberties Union (ACLU) sued Judge
Roy Moore of Gadsden, Alabama, for displaying the Ten Commandments in his courtroom. Such a display, the ACLU said, violates the
separation of church and state, which is guaranteed by the U.S.
Constitution. The voters, however, supported Moore. In 2000,
Moore was elected Chief Justice of the Alabama Supreme Court,
running on a promise to "restore the moral foundation of law." The
"Ten Commandments judge" thus became the most powerful jurist
in the state of Alabama.

Moore was not through making his point, however. In the wee
hours of July 31, 2001, he had a granite monument dedicated to the
Ten Commandments installed in the Alabama state judicial building.
This monument weighed over 5,000 pounds, and nobody entering the
building could miss it. So, Moore was sued again, and again the people
stood behind him: 77% of Americans supported his right to display the

t. Yet the law disagreed. When Moore ignored a court order
the monument, the Alabama Court of the Judiciary fired
ιg that he had placed himself above the law. Moore, however,
hat he was recognizing *God's* rightful place above the law.
.012, Moore was again elected Chief Justice of the Alabama
Court. When the U.S. Supreme Court ruled that same-sex
ιave the right to marry, Moore told Alabama judges that
they had a "ministerial duty" to ignore the ruling. Thus, in 2016,
Moore was again removed from office, in what he called "a politically
motivated effort by radical homosexual and transgender groups." In
2017, Moore almost became a U.S. senator, winning the Republican
primary but then losing to the Democrat after several women claimed
that Moore had molested them when they were teenagers.

Few Americans describe themselves as "atheists," but this may
be due to the social stigma of being seen as a non-believer; some people
might not want to admit it. In 2017, a study that measured religious
belief without asking people directly whether they believe, found that
26% of Americans do not believe in God. So, there might be a lot of
atheists out there. Nevertheless, the United States is a religious country.
The stigma that exists is directed at atheists, not at believers. When
asked directly, most Americans say that religion is "very important" in
their lives, and three-quarters say they're Christians.

Members of the Christian clergy are sometimes treated as
moral experts in America: Hospitals may ask them to sit on ethics
committees; reporters may interview them on the moral dimensions
of a story; and churchgoers look to them for guidance. The clergy
even help decide whether movies will be rated "G," "PG," "PG-13,"
"R," or "NC-17." Priests and ministers are assumed to be wise coun-
selors who often give sound moral advice.

Why are the clergy viewed in this way? The reason is not
that they have proven themselves to be better or wiser than other
people—as a group, they seem to be neither better nor worse than the
rest of us. There is a deeper reason why they are seen as having moral
insight. In popular thinking, morality and religion are inseparable;
people believe that morality can be understood only in the context of
religion. Thus, the clergy are assumed to be authorities on morality.

It is not hard to see why people think this. When viewed from
a nonreligious perspective, the universe seems to be a cold, mean-
ingless place, devoid of value and purpose. In Bertrand Russell's

essay "A Free Man's Worship" (1903), he expresses what he calls the "scientific" view of the world:

> That Man is the product of causes which had no prevision of the end they were achieving; that his origin, his growth, his hopes and fears, his loves and his beliefs, are but the outcome of accidental collocations of atoms; that no fire, no heroism, no intensity of thought and feeling, can preserve an individual life beyond the grave; that all the labours of the ages, all the devotion, all the inspiration, all the noonday brightness of human genius, are destined to extinction in the vast death of the solar system, and that the whole temple of Man's achievement must inevitably be buried beneath the debris of a universe in ruins—all these things, if not quite beyond dispute, are yet so nearly certain, that no philosophy which rejects them can hope to stand.

From a religious perspective, however, things look very different. Judaism and Christianity teach that the world was created by a loving, all-powerful God to provide a home for us. We, in turn, were created in his image, to be his children. Thus, the world is not devoid of meaning and purpose. It is, instead, the arena in which God's plans are realized. What could be more natural, then, than to think of "morality" as part of religion, while the atheist's world has no place for values?

4.2. The Divine Command Theory

Christians, Jews, and Muslims all believe that God has told us to obey certain rules of conduct. God does not force these rules on us. He created us as free agents; so, we may choose what to do. But if we live as we should, then we must follow God's laws. This idea has been expanded into a theory known as the Divine Command Theory. The basic idea is that God decrees what is right and wrong. Actions that God commands us to do are morally required; actions that God forbids us to do are morally wrong; and all other actions are morally neutral.

This theory has a number of advantages. For one, it immediately solves the old problem of the objectivity of ethics. Ethics is not merely a matter of personal feeling or social custom. Whether something is right or wrong is perfectly objective: It is right if God commands it and wrong if God forbids it. Moreover, the Divine Command Theory explains why any of us should bother with morality. Why shouldn't we just look out for ourselves? If immorality is the violation of God's commandments, then there is an easy answer: On the day of final reckoning, you will be held accountable.

There are, however, serious problems with the theory. Of course, atheists would not accept it, because they do not believe that God exists. But there are difficulties even for believers. The main problem was identified by Plato, a Greek philosopher who lived 400 years before Jesus of Nazareth. Plato's books were written as conversations, or dialogues, in which Plato's teacher Socrates is always the main speaker. In one of them, the *Euthyphro*, there is a discussion of whether "right" can be defined as "what the gods command." Socrates is skeptical and asks: Is conduct right because the gods command it, or do the gods command it because it is right? This is one of the most famous questions in the history of philosophy. The British philosopher Antony Flew (1923–2010) suggests that "one good test of a person's aptitude for philosophy is to discover whether he can grasp [the] force and point" of this question.

Socrates's question is about whether God *makes* the moral truths true or whether he merely *recognizes* their truth. There's a big difference between these options. I know that the Burj Khalifa building in the United Arab Emirates is the tallest building in the world; I recognize that fact. However, I did not make it true. Rather, it was made true by the designers and builders in the city of Dubai. Is God's relation to ethics like my relation to the Burj Khalifa building or like the relation of the builders? This question poses a dilemma, and each option leads to trouble.

First, we might say that *right conduct is right because God commands it.* For example, according to Exodus 20:16, God commands us to be truthful. Thus, we should be truthful simply because God requires it. God's command makes truthfulness right, just as the builders of a skyscraper make the building tall. This is the Divine Command Theory. It is almost the theory of Shakespeare's character Hamlet. Hamlet said that nothing is good or bad, but thinking makes it so. According to the Divine Command Theory, nothing is good or bad, except when *God's* thinking makes it so.

This idea encounters several difficulties.

1. *This conception of morality is mysterious.* What does it mean to say that God "makes" truthfulness right? It is easy enough to understand how physical objects are made, at least in principle. We have all made something, if only a sand castle or a peanut-butter-and-jelly sandwich. But making truthfulness right is not like that; it could not be done by rearranging things in the physical environment. How, then, could it be done? No one knows.

To see the problem, consider some wretched case of child abuse. On the Divine Command Theory, God could make *that* instance of child abuse right—not by turning a slap into a friendly pinch of the cheek, but *by commanding that the slap is right.* This proposal defies human understanding. How could merely saying, or commanding, that the slap is right make it right? If true, this conception of morality would be a mystery.

2. *This conception of morality makes God's commands arbitrary.* Suppose a parent forbids a teenager from doing something, and when the teenager asks why, the parent responds, "Because I said so!" In such a case, the parent seems to be imposing his will on the child arbitrarily. Yet the Divine Command Theory sees God as being like such a parent. Rather than offering a reason for his commands, God merely says, "Because I said so."

God's commands also seem arbitrary because he always could have commanded the opposite. For example, suppose God commands us to be truthful. On the Divine Command Theory, he just as easily could have commanded us to be liars, and then lying, and not truthfulness, would be right. After all, before God issues his commands, no reasons for or against lying exist—*because God is the one who creates the reasons.* So, from a moral point of view, God's commands are arbitrary. He could command anything whatsoever. This result may seem not only unacceptable but impious from a religious point of view.

3. *This conception of morality provides the wrong reasons for moral principles.* There are many things wrong with child abuse: It is malicious; it involves the unnecessary infliction of pain; it can have unwanted long-term psychological effects; and so on. However, the Divine Command Theory does not care about any of those things; it sees the maliciousness, the pain, and the long-term effects of child abuse as being morally irrelevant. All it cares about, in the end, is whether child abuse runs counter to God's commands.

There are two ways of confirming that something is wrong here. First, notice something that the theory implies: *If God didn't exist, then child abuse wouldn't be wrong.* After all, if God didn't exist, then God wouldn't have been around to make child abuse wrong. However, child abuse would still be malicious, so it would still be wrong. Thus, the Divine Command Theory fails. Second, bear in mind that even a religious person might be genuinely in doubt as to what God has commanded. After all, religious texts disagree with each other, and sometimes there seem to be inconsistencies even within a single text. So, a person might be in doubt as to what God's will really is. However, a person need not be in doubt as to whether child abuse is wrong. What God has commanded is one thing; whether hitting children is wrong is another.

There is a way to avoid these troublesome consequences. We can take the second of Socrates's options. We need not say that right conduct is right because God commands it. Instead, we may say that God commands us to do certain things *because they are right.* God, who is infinitely wise, recognizes that truthfulness is better than deceitfulness, just as he recognizes in Genesis that the light he sees is good. For this reason, God commands us to be truthful.

If we take this option, then we avoid the consequences that spoiled the first alternative. We needn't worry about how God makes it wrong to lie, because he doesn't. God's commands are not arbitrary; they are the result of his wisdom in knowing what is best. Also, we are not saddled with the wrong explanations for our moral principles; instead, we are free to appeal to whatever justifications of them seem appropriate.

Unfortunately, this second option has a different drawback. In taking it, we abandon the theological conception of right and wrong. When we say that God commands us to be truthful *because* truthfulness is right, we acknowledge a standard that is independent of God's will. The rightness exists prior to God's command and is the reason for it. Thus, if we want to know *why* we should be truthful, the reply "because God commands it" does not really tell us. We may still ask, "*Why* does God command it?" and the answer to *that* question will provide the ultimate reason.

Many religious people believe that they must accept a theological conception of right and wrong because it would be sacrilegious not to do so. They feel, somehow, that if they believe in God, then right and wrong must be understood in terms of God's wishes. Our arguments, however, suggest that the Divine Command Theory is not only untenable but impious. And, in fact, some of the greatest theologians have rejected the theory for just these reasons.

4.3. The Theory of Natural Law

In the history of Christian thought, the dominant theory of ethics is not the Divine Command Theory. That honor instead goes to the Theory of Natural Law. This theory has three main parts.

1. The Theory of Natural Law rests on a particular view of the world. On this view, the world has a rational order, with values and purposes built into its very nature. This idea comes from the Greeks, whose worldview dominated Western thinking for over 1,700 years. The Greeks believed that *everything in nature has a purpose.*

Aristotle (384-322 B.C.) built this idea into his system of thought. To understand anything, he said, four questions must be asked: What is it? What is it made of? How did it come to be? And what is it for? The answers might be: This is a knife; it is made of metal; it was made by a craftsman; and it is used for cutting. Aristotle assumed that the last question—What is it for?—could be asked of anything whatever. "Nature," he said, "belongs to the class of causes which act for the sake of something."

Obviously, knives have a purpose, because craftsmen build them with a purpose in mind. But what about natural objects that we do not make? Aristotle believed that they have purposes, too. One of his examples was that we have teeth so that we can chew. Biological examples are quite persuasive; each part of our bodies does seem, intuitively, to have a special purpose—our eyes are for seeing, our ears are for hearing, our skin exists to protect us, and so on. But Aristotle's claim was not limited to organic beings. According to him, *everything* has a purpose. To take a different sort of example, he thought that rain falls so that plants can grow. He considered alternatives. For example, he asked whether the rain might fall "of necessity," which helps the plants only "by coincidence." However, he considered that unlikely.

The world, Aristotle thought, is an orderly, rational system in which each thing has a proper place and serves its own special purpose. There is a neat hierarchy: The rain exists for the sake of the plants, the plants exist for the sake of the animals, and the animals exist—of course—for the sake of people. Aristotle says, "If then we are right in believing that nature makes nothing without some end in view, nothing to no purpose, it must be that nature has made all things specifically for the sake of man." This worldview is stunningly anthropocentric, or human-centered. But Aristotle was hardly alone in having such thoughts; almost every important thinker in human history has advanced such a thesis. Humans are a remarkably vain species.

The Christian thinkers who came later found this worldview appealing. Only one thing was missing: God. Thus, the Christian thinkers said that the rain falls to help the plants *because that is what God intended*, and the animals are for human use because *that is what God made them for*. Values and purposes were thus seen as part of God's plan.

2. A corollary to this way of thinking is that the "laws of nature" describe not only how things *are* but also how things *ought to be*. The world is in harmony when things serve their natural purposes. When they do not, or cannot, things have gone wrong. Eyes that cannot see are defective, and drought is a natural evil; the badness of both is explained by reference to natural law. But there are also implications for human conduct. Moral rules are now viewed as deriving from the laws of nature. Some ways of behaving are said to be "natural" while others are regarded as "unnatural"; and "unnatural" acts are seen as morally wrong.

Consider, for example, the duty of beneficence. We are morally required to care about our neighbors. Why? According to the Theory of Natural Law, beneficence is natural for us, given the kind of creatures we are. We are by nature social and need the company of other people. Someone who does not care at all about others—who really does not care, through and through—is seen as deranged. Modern psychiatry says that such people suffer from *antisocial personality disorder*, and such people are commonly called *psychopaths* or *sociopaths*.

A callous personality is defective, just as eyes are defective if they cannot see. And, it may be added, this is true because we were created by God, with a specific "human" nature, as part of his overall plan.

The endorsement of beneficence is relatively uncontroversial. Natural-law theory has also been used, however, to support more questionable ideas. Religious thinkers often condemn "deviant" sexual practices, and they usually justify this by appealing to the Theory of Natural Law. If everything has a purpose, what is the purpose of sex? The obvious answer is procreation. Sexual activity that is not connected with making babies can, therefore, be seen as "unnatural," and practices like masturbation and gay sex may be condemned for this reason. This view of sex dates back at least to Saint Augustine (A.D. 354–430) and is explicit in the writings of Saint Thomas Aquinas (1225–1274). The moral theology of the Catholic Church is based on natural-law theory.

3. The third part concerns moral knowledge. How can we tell right from wrong? On the Divine Command Theory, we must consult God's commandments. On the Theory of Natural Law, however, the "natural laws" of morality are just laws of reason; so, what's right is what's supported by the best arguments. On this view, we can figure out what's right because God has given us the ability to reason. Moreover, God has given this ability to everyone, putting the believer and nonbeliever in the same position.

Objections to Natural-Law Theory. Outside the Catholic Church, the Theory of Natural Law has few advocates today. It is generally rejected for three reasons.

First, the idea that "what's natural is good" seems open to obvious counterexamples. Sometimes what's natural is bad. People naturally care much more about themselves than about strangers, but this is regrettable. Disease occurs naturally, but disease is bad. Children are naturally self-centered, but parents don't think this is a good thing.

Second, the Theory of Natural Law seems to confuse "is" and "ought." In the 18th century, David Hume pointed out that *what is the case* and *what ought to be the case* are logically different notions, and no conclusion about one follows from the other. We can say that people are naturally disposed to be beneficent, but it does not follow that they *ought* to be beneficent. Similarly, it may be true that sex produces babies, but it does not follow that sex *ought* or *ought not* to be engaged in only for that purpose. Facts are one thing; values are another.

Third, the Theory of Natural Law is now widely rejected because its view of the world conflicts with modern science. The world as described by Galileo, Newton, and Darwin has no need for "facts" about right and wrong. Their explanations of nature make no reference to values or purposes. What happens just happens, due to the laws of cause and effect. If the rain benefits the plants, this is because the plants have evolved by the laws of natural selection in a rainy climate.

Thus, modern science gives us a picture of the world as a realm of facts, where the only "natural laws" are the laws of physics, chemistry, and biology, working blindly and without purpose. Whatever values may be, they are not part of the natural order. As for the idea that "nature has made all things specifically for the sake of man," well, that was only vanity. To the extent that one accepts the worldview of modern science, one will reject the worldview of natural-law theory. That theory was a product, not of modern thought, but of the Middle Ages.

4.4. Religion and Particular Moral Issues

Some religious people will find the preceding discussion unsatisfying. It will seem too abstract to have any bearing on their actual lives. For them, the connection between morality and religion is an immediate, practical matter that centers on particular moral issues. It doesn't matter whether right and wrong are understood in terms of God's will or whether moral laws are laws of nature. What matters are the moral teachings of one's religion. The Scriptures and the church leaders are regarded as authorities; if one is truly faithful, one must accept what they say. Many Christians, for example, believe that they must oppose abortion because the church condemns it and because (they assume) the Scriptures do too.

Are there distinctively religious positions on major moral issues that believers must accept? The rhetoric of the pulpit suggests so. But there is good reason to think otherwise.

For one thing, it is often difficult to find specific moral guidance in the Scriptures. We face different problems than our ancestors faced 2,000 years ago; thus, the Scriptures may be silent on matters that seem pressing to us. The Bible does contain a number of general precepts—for example, to love one's neighbor and to treat others as one wishes to be treated. And those are fine principles, which have practical application in our lives. However, it is not clear what they imply about the rights of workers, or the extinction of species, or the funding of medical research, and so on.

Another problem is that the Scriptures and church tradition are often ambiguous. Authorities disagree, leaving the believer in the awkward position of having to choose which part of the tradition to accept. For instance, the New Testament condemns being rich, and there is a long tradition of self-denial and charitable giving that affirms this teaching. But there is also an obscure Old Testament figure named Jabez who asked God to "enlarge my territories" (1 Chronicles 4:10), and God did. A recent book urging Christians to adopt Jabez as their model became a best seller.

Thus, when people say that their moral views come from their religion, they are often mistaken. Really, they are making up their own minds about the issues and then interpreting the Scriptures, or church tradition, in a way that supports the conclusions they've already reached. Of course, this does not happen in every case, but it seems fair to say that it happens a lot. The question of wealth is one example; abortion is another.

In the debate over abortion, religious issues are never far from the discussion. Religious conservatives hold that the fetus is a person from the moment of conception, and so abortion is murder. The fetus, they believe, is not merely a *potential* person but is an *actual* person, possessing a full-fledged right to life. Liberals, of course, deny this—they say that the fetus is something less than that, at least early in the pregnancy.

The abortion issue is complex, but we are concerned only with how it relates to religion. Conservatives sometimes say that fetal life is sacred. Is that the Christian view? *Must* Christians condemn abortion? To answer those questions, one might look to the Scriptures or to church tradition.

The Scriptures. It is difficult to derive a prohibition against abortion from either the Jewish or the Christian Scriptures. The Scriptures never condemn abortion by name. However, conservatives sometimes quote certain passages that seem to suggest that fetuses have full human status. One of the most frequently cited passages is from the first chapter of Jeremiah, in which Jeremiah quotes God as saying, "Before I formed you in the womb I knew you, and before you were born I consecrated you." These words are presented as though they were God's endorsement of the conservative position: it is wrong to kill the unborn because the unborn are consecrated to God.

In context, however, these words obviously mean something different. Suppose we read the whole passage in which they occur:

> Now the word of the Lord came to me, saying, "Before I formed you in the womb I knew you, and before you were born I consecrated you; I appointed you a prophet to the nations."
>
> Then I said, "Ah, Lord God! Behold, I do not know how to speak, for I am only a youth." But the Lord said to me,
>
> "Do not say, 'I am only a youth'; for to all to whom I send you, you shall go, and whatever I command you, you shall speak. Be not afraid of them, for I am with you to deliver you."

This passage has nothing to do with abortion. Instead, Jeremiah is asserting his authority as a prophet. He is saying, in effect, "God told me to speak for him. I tried to say no, but he insisted." However, Jeremiah puts this point poetically; he says that God selected him to be a prophet even before he was born.

The pattern here is familiar: Someone who is advocating a moral position quotes a few words from the Bible, out of context, and then interprets them in a way that supports their position; yet those words suggest something else entirely when read in context. When this happens, is it accurate to say that the person is "following the moral teachings of the Bible"? Or is it accurate to say that he has searched the Bible to find support for something he already believes, and has interpreted the Bible with this in mind? The latter, when true, suggests an especially arrogant attitude—the attitude that God himself must share one's opinions!

Three other biblical passages support a *liberal* view of abortion. A woman who has recently had sex might be pregnant. Yet three times the Bible recommends executing women for having sex outside of marriage, without suggesting that the executioners wait until they can be sure that the woman isn't pregnant (Genesis 38:24; Leviticus 21:9; Deuteronomy 22:20–21). This suggests that the death of the fetus doesn't matter—that the fetus has no right to life.

Church Tradition. Today, the Catholic Church strongly opposes abortion. In many Protestant churches, too, abortion is routinely denounced from the pulpit. Many people of faith, therefore, feel they must condemn abortion "for religious reasons," no matter how Scripture is interpreted. What lies behind the Church's anti-abortion stance?

To some extent, the Vatican has always opposed abortion for the same reason that it condemns condoms, birth control pills, and other forms of contraception: All of these activities interfere with natural processes. According to natural-law theory, sex is supposed to lead to the birth of a healthy baby. Condoms and birth control pills prevent this from happening by preventing pregnancy; abortion prevents it by killing the fetus. Thus, by the lights of traditional Catholic thinking, abortion is wrong because it disrupts a natural process. This type of argument, however, can hardly show that Christians "must" oppose abortion. It depends on natural-law theory, which, as we have seen, predates modern science. Yet Christians today need not reject modern science—even the Catholic Church dropped its opposition to Charles Darwin's theory of evolution back in 1950. Thus, Christians are not required to oppose abortion based on natural-law considerations.

At any rate, to say that abortion interferes with a natural process is to say nothing about the moral status of the fetus. Recent popes have not merely believed that abortion is immoral, like using a condom; they have believed it to be *murder.* How did this position become dominant within the Catholic Church? Have Church leaders always regarded the fetus as enjoying a special moral status?

For most of the Church's history—until around A.D. 1200—little of relevance is known. Back then, there were no universities, and the Church was not especially intellectual. People believed all kinds of things, for all kinds of reasons. But then, in the 13th century, Saint

Thomas Aquinas constructed a philosophical system that became the bedrock of later Catholic thought. The key question, he believed, is whether the fetus has a soul: If it does, then abortion is murder; if it doesn't, then abortion is not murder. Does the fetus have a soul? Aquinas accepted Aristotle's idea that the soul is the "substantial form" of man. Let's not worry about what that means, exactly; what's important is that human beings are supposed to acquire a "substantial form" when their bodies take on human shape. So now the key question is: When do human beings first look human?

When a baby is born, anyone can see that it has a human shape. In Aquinas's day, however, nobody knew when fetuses begin to look like that—after all, fetal development occurs out of sight, in the mother's womb. Aristotle had believed, for no good reason, that males acquire a soul 40 days after conception and females do after 90 days. Presumably, many Christians accepted this view. (Aquinas himself so respected Aristotle that he always referred to him as just "the Philosopher.") At any rate, for the next several centuries, most Catholic thinkers strongly opposed abortion *throughout* pregnancy, because, at any moment, the fetus might have *already* acquired a human form—and so, killing the fetus might be murder.

Contrary to popular belief, the Catholic Church has never officially maintained that the fetus acquires a soul at the moment of conception. Around 1600, however, some theologians began to say that the soul enters the body a few days after conception, and so abortion is murder early on. This monumental change in Catholic thinking occurred without much debate. Maybe the issue seemed unimportant because the Church already opposed early-term abortions. At any rate, we know little about what happened.

Today we know a lot about fetal development. We know, through microscopes and ultrasounds, that fetuses do not look human until several weeks into the pregnancy. Thus, a follower of Aquinas should now say that fetuses have no soul during the first month or two of pregnancy. However, there has been no movement inside the Catholic Church to adopt that position. For reasons that remain murky, the Church adopted a conservative view of the fetus in the 1600s, and it has maintained that view ever since.

The purpose of reviewing this history is not to suggest that the contemporary church's position is wrong. For all I have said, it may be right. The point, rather, is this: every generation interprets its traditions to support its favored moral views. To illustrate this, we could have also discussed the church's shifting views on slavery, or capital punishment, or the status of women. In each case, the moral stance taken by the Church seems not to be derived from the Bible so much as imposed on it, in different ways at different times. If we look at the *whole* history of Christianity, then we find little reason to oppose abortion.

This chapter has argued for several conclusions: that right and wrong are not to be understood in terms of God's will; that morality is a matter of reason and conscience, not religious faith; and that, in any case, religious considerations do not provide definitive solutions to many of the moral problems we face. Together, these conclusions point to a larger conclusion: that morality and religion are, in a word, different.

Of course, religious beliefs can bear on moral issues. Consider, for example, the doctrine of eternal life. If some people go to heaven when they die—and so, death is a good thing for them—then this might affect the morality of killing these people. Or suppose we believe, upon studying ancient prophecies, that supernatural forces will soon bring the world to a fiery end. If so, then this might reduce our fear of climate change. The relationship between morality and religion is complicated, but it is a relationship between two different subjects.

This conclusion may seem antireligious. However, it has not been reached by questioning the validity of religion. The arguments we have considered do not assume that Christianity or any other theological system is false; they merely show that, even if such a system is true, morality remains a separate matter.

Notes on Sources

77% of Americans support Judge Roy Moore: Gallup Poll, September 2003. For Moore's remark about the homosexual and transgender conspiracy, see Campbell Robertson, "Roy Moore, Alabama Chief Justice, Suspended over Gay Marriage Order," *The New York Times*, September 30, 2016.

26% of Americans might be atheists: Will M. Gervais and Maxine B. Najle, "How Many Atheists Are There?" (last edited on March 31, 2017) at psyarxiv.com.

53% of Americans say that religion is "very important" in their lives, and 74% identify as Christian: Gallup Poll, December 2016. On the clergy's role in assigning movie ratings, see the documentary *This Film Is Not Yet Rated* (2006).

Bertrand Russell is quoted from pp. 45–46 of "A Free Man's Worship" (1903) in *Mysticism and Logic* (Garden City, NY: Doubleday, Anchor Books, n.d.).

Antony Flew's remark about philosophical talent is on p. 109 of *God and Philosophy* (New York: Dell, 1966).

Hamlet's exact words were: "Why, then 'tis none to you; for there is nothing either good or bad, but thinking makes it so: to me it is a prison" (act 2, scene 2, lines 254–256 of *The Tragedy of Hamlet, Prince of Denmark*, in *The Complete Works of William Shakespeare* [USA: Octopus Books, 1985, p. 844]).

Aristotle is quoted from *The Basic Works of Aristotle*, edited by Richard McKeon (New York: Random House, 1941), p. 249 ("Nature belongs to the class of causes": *Physics* 2.8, 198b10–11), and from *The Politics*, translated by T. A. Sinclair (Harmondsworth, Middlesex: Penguin Books, 1962), p. 40 ("If then we are right in believing": I.8, 1256b20).

Saint Thomas Aquinas is quoted from the *Summa Theologica*, III *Quodlibet*, 27, translated by Thomas Gilby in *St. Thomas Aquinas: Philosophical Texts* (New York: Oxford University Press, 1960).

The passage supposedly about abortion is Jeremiah 1:4–8. I quoted the English Standard Version translation of *The Holy Bible* (2001).

On the history of Catholic thought, see John Connery, SJ, *Abortion: The Development of the Roman Catholic Perspective* (Chicago: Loyola University Press, 1977) (the Church has never said that the fetus acquires a soul at conception: p. 308). I am grateful to Steve Sverdlik for tutoring me in this area.

The Catholic Church officially softened its stance on evolution with Pope Pius XII's encyclical *Humani Generis* (1950).

CHAPTER 5

*E*thical Egoism

The achievement of his own happiness is man's highest moral purpose.
AYN RAND, *THE VIRTUE OF SELFISHNESS* (1961)

5.1. Is There a Duty to Help the Starving?

Each year millions of people die from health problems brought on by malnutrition. Often, those who die are children. Every day, around 15,800 children under the age of five die, almost always from preventable causes. That comes to around 5.9 million deaths each year. Even if this estimate is too high, the number who die unnecessarily is staggering.

Poverty poses an acute problem for many of us who are much better off. We spend money on ourselves, not only on necessities but on luxuries—jewelry, travel, the latest smartphone, and so on. In America, even people with modest incomes sometimes enjoy such things. But we could forgo our luxuries and give the money for famine relief instead. The fact that we *don't* suggests that we regard our luxuries as more important than the lives of the starving.

Why do we let people die of hunger when we could save them? Few of us actually believe our luxuries are that important. Most of us, if asked directly, would feel embarrassed, and we might say that we should do more to help. One reason we don't is that we rarely think about it. Living our own comfortable lives, we are insulated from the realities of poverty. The people starving are at some distance from us; we do not see them, and we can avoid thinking about them. And when we do think about them, it is only abstractly, as statistics. Unfortunately for the hungry, statistics have little power to move us.

We respond differently when there is a "crisis," as when Hurricane Harvey dumped fifty inches of rain onto Houston over four days, and millions of people had to flee their homes. Then the horrors are newsworthy, and relief efforts are mobilized. But when the suffering is scattered, the situation seems less pressing. The 5.9 million children who die each year might all be saved if they were gathered in, say, Chicago.

But leaving aside the question of why we behave as we do, what is our duty? What *should* we do? Common sense might tell us to balance our own interests against the interests of others. It is understandable, of course, that we look out for ourselves, and no one can be blamed for attending to her own basic needs. But at the same time, the needs of others are important, and when we can help others—especially at little cost to ourselves—we should do so. So, if you have an extra $10, and giving it to charity would help save a child's life, then common sense would say that you should do so.

This way of thinking assumes that we have duties to others simply because *they could be helped or harmed by what we do.* If a certain action would benefit (or harm) other people, then that is a reason why we should (or should not) perform that action. The commonsense assumption is that other people's interests *count*, from a moral point of view.

But one person's common sense is another person's naïve platitude. Some people believe that we have no duties to others. On their view, known as Ethical Egoism, each person ought to pursue his or her own self-interest exclusively. This is the morality of selfishness. It holds that our only duty is to do what is best for ourselves. Other people matter only insofar as they can benefit us.

5.2. Psychological Egoism

Before we discuss Ethical Egoism, we should discuss a theory it is often confused with—Psychological Egoism. Ethical Egoism claims that each person *ought* to pursue his or her own self-interest exclusively. Psychological Egoism, by contrast, asserts that each person *does in fact* pursue his or her own self-interest exclusively. These theories are very different. It is one thing to say that people are self-interested and that our neighbors will not give to charity. It is quite another thing to say that people *ought* to be self-interested and that our neighbors *ought* not to give to charity. Psychological Egoism makes a claim about human nature, or about the way things are; Ethical Egoism makes a claim about morality, or about the way things should be.

Psychological Egoism is not a theory of ethics; rather, it is a theory of human psychology. But ethicists have always worried about it. If Psychological Egoism were true, then moral philosophy would seem pointless. After all, if people are going to behave self-ishly *no matter what*, then what's the point of discussing what they "ought" to do? Whatever it is they "ought" to do, they aren't going to do it. It might be naïve of us to think that our moral theories can matter in the real world.

Is Altruism Possible? In 1939, when World War II began, Raoul Wallenberg was an unknown businessman living in Sweden. During the war, Sweden was a good place to be. As a neutral country, it was never bombed, blockaded, or invaded. Yet, in 1944, Wallenberg voluntarily left Sweden for Nazi-controlled Hungary. Officially, he would just be another Swedish diplomat in Budapest. But his real mission was to save lives. In Hungary, Hitler had begun implementing his "final solution to the Jewish problem": Jews were being rounded up, deported, and then murdered at Nazi killing stations. Wallenberg wanted to stop the slaughter.

Wallenberg did help to persuade the Hungarian government to halt the deportations. However, the Hungarian government was soon replaced by a Nazi puppet regime, and the mass killing resumed. Wallenberg then issued "Swedish Protective Passes" to thousands of Jews, insisting that they all had connections to Sweden and were under the protection of his government. Wallenberg also helped many people hide. When these people were discovered, he would stand between them and the Nazis, telling the Germans that they would have to shoot him first. All in all, he saved thousands of human lives. At the end of the war, Wallenberg stayed in Hungary, amid the chaos, as most other diplomats fled. He then disappeared, and for a long time his fate was unknown. Now we believe he was killed, not by the Germans, but by the Soviets, who imprisoned him after taking over Hungary. Wallenberg's body was never found, and the Swedish government did not officially declare him to be dead until 2016.

Wallenberg's story is especially dramatic, but it is not unique. The Israeli government recognizes over 22,000 Gentiles who risked their lives trying to save Jews from being murdered in the Holocaust. The Israelis call these heroic individuals "The Righteous among the Nations." And though few of us have saved lives, acts of altruism appear to be common. People do favors for one another. They give blood. They build homeless shelters. They volunteer in hospitals. They read to the blind. Many people give money to worthy causes. In some cases, the amount given is extraordinary. Warren Buffett, an American businessman, gave $37 billion to the Bill and Melinda Gates Foundation to promote global health and education. Zell Kravinsky, an American real estate investor, gave his entire $45-million fortune to charity. And then, for good measure, he donated one of his kidneys to a complete stranger. Oseola McCarty, an 87-year-old African-American woman from Hattiesburg, Mississippi, gave $150,000 to endow a scholarship fund at the University of Southern Mississippi. For 75 years, she had saved up money, working as a maid. She never owned a car, and at the age of 87, she still walked over a mile to the nearest grocery store, pushing her own shopping cart.

These are remarkable deeds, but should they be taken at face value? According to Psychological Egoism, we may see ourselves as noble and self-sacrificing, but really we are not. In reality, we care only for ourselves. Could this theory be true? Why have people believed it, in the face of so much contrary evidence? Two arguments are often given for Psychological Egoism.

The Argument That We Always Do What We Want to Do. "Every act you have ever performed since the day you were born was performed because you wanted something." So wrote Dale Carnegie, the author of the first and best self-help book, *How to Win Friends and Influence People* (1936). Carnegie thought of desire as the key to human psychology. If he was correct, then when we describe one person's action as altruistic and another person's action as self-interested, we may be overlooking the fact that in each case *the person is merely doing what he or she most wants to do.* For example, if Raoul Wallenberg chose to go to Hungary, then he wanted to go there more than he wanted to remain in Sweden—and why should he be praised for altruism when he was only doing what he wanted to do? His action sprang from his own wishes, from his own sense of what he wanted. Thus, he was moved by his own self-interest. And because the same may be said about any alleged act of kindness, we can conclude that Psychological Egoism must be true.

This argument, however, is flawed. There are things that we do, not because we want to, but because we feel that we *ought* to. For example, I may write my grandmother a letter because I promised my mother I would, even though I don't want to do it. It is sometimes suggested that we do such things because we most want to keep our promises. But that is not true. It is simply false to say that my strongest desire is to keep my promise. What I most want is to break my promise, but I don't, as a matter of conscience. For all we know, Wallenberg was in this position: Perhaps he wanted to stay in Sweden, but he felt that he had to go to Hungary to save lives. In any case, the fact that he chose to go does not imply that he most wanted to do so.

The argument has a second flaw. Suppose we concede that we always act on our strongest desires. Even if this were so, it would not follow that Wallenberg acted out of self-interest. For if Wallenberg wanted to help others, even at great risk to himself, then that is precisely what makes his behavior altruistic. The mere fact that you act on your own desires does not mean that you are looking out for yourself; it all depends on *what* you desire. If you care only about yourself and give no thought to others, then you are acting out of self-interest; but if you want other people to be happy, and you act on that desire, then you are not. To put the point another way: In assessing whether an action is self-interested, the issue is not *whether* the action is based on a desire; the issue is *what kind of desire it is based on*. If you want to help someone else, then your motive is altruistic, not self-interested.

Therefore, this argument goes wrong in every way it could: The premise is not true—we don't always do what we most want to do—and even if it were true, the conclusion would not follow from it.

The Argument That We Always Do What Makes Us Feel Good. The second argument for Psychological Egoism appeals to the fact that so-called altruistic actions produce a sense of self-satisfaction in the person who performs them. Acting "unselfishly" makes people feel good about themselves, and that is why they do it.

According to a 19th-century newspaper, this argument was made by Abraham Lincoln. The Springfield, Illinois, *Monitor* reported,

> Mr. Lincoln once remarked to a fellow-passenger on an old-time mud coach that all men were prompted by selfishness in doing good. His fellow-passenger was antagonizing this position when they were passing over a corduroy bridge that spanned a slough. As they crossed this bridge they espied an old razor-backed sow on the bank making a terrible noise because her pigs had got into the slough and were in danger of drowning. As the old coach began to climb the hill, Mr. Lincoln called out, "Driver, can't you stop just a moment?" Then Mr. Lincoln jumped out, ran back, and lifted the little pigs out of the mud and water and placed them on the bank. When he returned, his companion remarked: "Now, Abe, where does selfishness come in on this little episode?" "Why, bless your soul, Ed, that was the very essence of selfishness. I should have had no peace of mind all day had I gone on and left that suffering old sow worrying over those pigs. I did it to get peace of mind, don't you see?"

In this story, Honest Abe employs a time-honored tactic of Psychological Egoism: *the strategy of reinterpreting motives*. Everyone knows that people sometimes seem to act altruistically; but if we look deeper, we may find that something else is going on. And usually it is not hard to discover that the "unselfish" behavior is actually connected to some benefit for the person who does it. Thus, Lincoln talks about the peace of mind he got from rescuing the pigs.

Other examples of alleged altruism can also be reinterpreted. According to some of Raoul Wallenberg's friends, he was depressed before he went to Hungary, feeling like his life wasn't amounting to much. So he undertook deeds that would make him a heroic figure. His quest for a more significant life was spectacularly successful—here we are, more than 60 years after his death, talking about him. Mother Teresa, the nun who spent her life working among the poor in Calcutta, is often cited as a perfect example of altruism—but, of course, she believed that she would be handsomely rewarded in heaven. And as for Zell Kravinsky, who gave away both his fortune and a kidney, his parents never gave him much praise, so he was always trying to do things that even they would admire. Kravinsky himself said that, as he began to give away his money, he came to think of a donation as "a treat to myself. I really thought of it as something pleasurable."

Despite all this, Lincoln's argument is flawed. It may be true that one of his motives in saving the pigs was to preserve his own peace of mind. *But the fact that Lincoln had a self-interested motive doesn't mean that he didn't have benevolent motives as well.* In fact, Lincoln's desire to help the pigs might have been even greater than his desire to preserve his peace of mind. And if this isn't true in Lincoln's case, it will be true in other cases: If I see a child drowning, my desire to help that child will usually be greater than my desire to avoid a guilty conscience. Cases like these are counterexamples to Psychological Egoism.

In some instances of altruism, we may have *no* self-interested motives. For example, in 2007, a 50-year-old construction worker named Wesley Autrey was waiting for a subway train in New York City. Autrey saw a man near him collapse, his body convulsing. The man got up, only to stumble to the edge of the platform and fall onto the train tracks. At that moment, the headlights of a train appeared. "I had to make a split[-second] decision," Autrey later said. He then leapt onto the tracks and lay on top of the man, pressing him down into a space a foot deep. The train's brakes screeched, but it could not stop in time. People on the platform screamed. Five cars passed over the men, smudging Autrey's blue knit cap with grease. When onlookers realized that both men were safe, they broke out into applause. "I just saw someone who needed help," Autrey later said. He had saved the man's life, never giving a thought to his own well-being.

There is a general lesson to be learned here, having to do with the nature of desire. We want all sorts of things—money, friends, fame, a new car, and so on—and because we desire these things, we may derive satisfaction from getting them. But the object of our desire is typically *not* the feeling of satisfaction—that is not what we are after. What we want is simply the money, the friends, the fame, and the car. It is the same with helping others. Our desire to help others often comes first; the good feelings we get may merely be a by-product.

Conclusion about Psychological Egoism. If Psychological Egoism is so implausible, why have so many intelligent people been attracted to it? Some people like the theory's cynical view of human nature. Others may like its simplicity. And, indeed, it would be pleasing if a single factor could explain all human behavior. But human beings seem too complicated for that. Psychological Egoism is not a credible theory.

Thus, morality has nothing to fear from Psychological Egoism. Given that we *can* be moved by regard for our neighbors, it is not pointless to talk about whether we *should* help them. Moral theorizing need not be a naïve endeavor, based on an unrealistic view of human nature.

5.3. Three Arguments for Ethical Egoism

Ethical Egoism, again, is the doctrine that each person ought to pursue his or her own self-interest exclusively. This is not the commonsense view that one should promote one's own interests *in addition to* the interests of others. Ethical Egoism is the radical idea that the principle of self-interest accounts for *all* of one's obligations.

However, Ethical Egoism does not tell you to *avoid* helping others. Sometimes your interests will coincide with the well-being of others, so you'll help yourself by helping them. For example, if you can convince your teacher to cancel the assignment, this will benefit you *and* your classmates. Ethical Egoism does not forbid such actions; in fact, it may recommend them. The theory insists only that the benefit to others is not what makes the act right. Rather, the act is right because it benefits you.

Nor does Ethical Egoism imply that in pursuing your interests, you should always do what you want to, or what offers you the most short-term pleasure. Someone may want to smoke cigarettes, or bet all his money at the racetrack, or set up a meth lab in his basement. Ethical Egoism would frown on all of these actions, despite their possible short-term benefits. Ethical Egoism says that a person ought to do what really is in his or her own best interests, over the long run. It endorses selfishness, not foolishness.

Now let's discuss the three main arguments for Ethical Egoism.

The Argument That Altruism Is Self-Defeating. The first argument has several variations:

- Everyone is aware of his or her own wants and needs. More-over, each of us is uniquely placed to pursue those wants and needs effectively. At the same time, we understand other people only imperfectly, and we are not well placed to advance their interests. For these reasons, if we try to be "our brother's keeper," we will often bungle the job and do more harm than good.
- At the same time, the policy of "looking out for others" is an offensive intrusion into other people's privacy; it is essentially a policy of minding other people's business.
- Making other people the object of one's "charity" is degrading to them: it robs them of their dignity and self-respect, and it says to them, in effect, that they are not competent to care for themselves. Moreover, such a policy is self-fulfilling: those who are "helped" cease to be self-reliant and become passively dependent on others. That is why the recipients of charity are often resentful rather than appreciative.

In each case, the policy of "looking out for others" is said to be self-defeating. If we want to do what is best for people, we should not adopt so-called altruistic policies. On the contrary, if each person looks after his or her own interests, everyone will be better off.

It is possible to object to this argument on a number of grounds. Of course, no one favors bungling, butting in, or depriving people of their self-respect. But is that really what's going on when we feed hungry children? Is the starving child in Somalia really harmed when we "intrude" into "her business" by giving her food? It hardly seems likely. Yet we can set this point aside, for this way of thinking has an even more serious defect.

The trouble is that it isn't really an argument for Ethical Egoism at all. The argument concludes that we should adopt certain policies of behavior, and those policies may appear to be egoistic. However, the *reason* we should adopt those policies is decidedly unegoistic. It is said that adopting those policies will promote the betterment of society—but according to Ethical Egoism, we shouldn't care about that. Spelled out fully, the argument says:

(1) We ought to do whatever will best promote everyone's interests.

(2) The best way to promote everyone's interests is for each of us to pursue our own interests exclusively.

(3) Therefore, each of us should pursue our own interests exclusively.

If we accept this reasoning, then we are not Ethical Egoists. Even though we might behave like egoists, our ultimate principle is one of beneficence—we are trying to help everyone, and not just ourselves. Rather than being egoists, we turn out to be altruists with a peculiar view of what promotes the general welfare.

Ayn Rand's Argument. Philosophers don't pay much attention to the work of Ayn Rand (1905-1982). The major themes in her novels— the primacy of the individual and the superiority of capitalism—are developed more rigorously by other writers. Yet she was a charismatic figure who attracted a devoted following. Ethical Egoism is associated more with her than with any other 20th-century writer.

Ayn Rand regarded the "ethics of altruism" as a totally destructive idea, both in society as a whole and in the lives of those taken in by it. Altruism, she thought, leads to a denial of the value of the individual. It says to a person: Your life is merely something to be sacrificed. "If a man accepts the ethics of altruism," she writes, "his first concern is not how to live his life, but how to sacrifice it." Those who promote the ethics of altruism are beneath contempt— they are parasites. Rather than working to build and sustain their own lives, they leech off those who do. Rand continues,

> Parasites, moochers, looters, brutes and thugs can be of no value to a human being—nor can he gain any benefit from living in a society geared to *their* needs, demands and protections, a

society that treats him as a sacrificial animal and penalizes him for his virtues in order to reward *them* for their vices, which means: a society based on the ethics of altruism.

By "sacrificing one's life," Rand does not mean anything so dramatic as dying. A person's life consists, in part, of projects undertaken and goods earned and created. Thus, to demand that a person abandon his projects and give up his goods is to demand that he "sacrifice his life."

Rand also suggests that there is a metaphysical basis for Ethical Egoism. Somehow, it is the only ethic that takes seriously the *reality* of the individual person. She bemoans "the enormity of the extent to which altruism erodes men's capacity to grasp . . . the value of an individual life; it reveals a mind from which the reality of a human being has been wiped out."

What, then, of the hungry children? It might be said that Ethical Egoism itself "reveals a mind from which the reality of a human being has been wiped out," namely, the human being who is starving. But Rand quotes with approval the answer given by one of her followers: "Once, when Barbara Brandon was asked by a student: 'What will happen to the poor . . . ?' she answered: 'If *you* want to help them, you will not be stopped.'"

All these remarks are part of a single argument that goes something like this:

(1) Each person has only one life to live. If we value the individual, then we must agree that this life is of supreme importance. After all, it is all one has, and all one is.

(2) The ethics of altruism regards the life of the individual as something to be sacrificed for the good of others. Therefore, the ethics of altruism does not take seriously the value of the individual.

(3) Ethical Egoism, which allows each person to view his or her own life as having supreme value, does take the individual seriously—it is, in fact, the only philosophy that does.

(4) Thus, we should accept Ethical Egoism.

One problem with this argument, as you may have noticed, is its assumption that we have only two options: Either we accept the ethics of altruism, or we accept Ethical Egoism. The choice is then made to look obvious by depicting altruism as an idea that only an idiot would accept. The ethics of altruism is said to be the view that one's own interests have *no* value and that we must be ready to sacrifice ourselves *totally* whenever *anybody* asks us to. If this is altruism, then any other view, including Ethical Egoism, will look good by comparison.

But that is hardly a fair picture of the options. What we called the commonsense view stands between the two extremes. It says that one's own interests *and* the interests of others are important, and so we must strike a balance between them. Sometimes, one should act for the sake of others; at other times, one should look after oneself. Even if we reject the extreme ethics of altruism, we needn't embrace the extreme of Ethical Egoism. There is a middle ground.

Ethical Egoism as Compatible with Commonsense Morality. The third argument takes a different approach. Ethical Egoism is usually presented as challenging common sense. It is possible, however, to interpret it as *supporting* our commonsense moral view.

This interpretation goes as follows: Ordinary morality consists in obeying certain rules. We must speak the truth, keep our promises, avoid harming others, and so on. At first, these duties seem to have nothing in common—they are just a bunch of discrete rules. Yet there may be a unity to them. Ethical Egoists would say that all these duties spring from the one fundamental principle of self-interest.

Understood in this way, Ethical Egoism is not such a radical doctrine. It does not challenge ordinary morality; it only tries to explain and systematize it. And it does a surprisingly good job. It can provide plausible explanations of the duties mentioned above, and more:

- *The duty not to harm others:* If we do things that harm other people, other people won't mind harming us. We won't have friends; we will be shunned and despised; and we won't get help when we need it. If our offenses are serious enough, we might wind up in jail. Thus, it benefits us not to harm others.
- *The duty not to lie:* If we lie to other people, we will suffer all the ill effects of a bad reputation. People will distrust us

and avoid doing business with us. People will be dishonest with us once they realize that we have been dishonest with them. Thus, we benefit from being truthful.

- *The duty to keep our promises:* It is to our own advantage to enter into mutually beneficial arrangements with other people. To benefit from those arrangements, we need to be able to rely on others to keep their word. But we can hardly expect them to do that if we do not keep our promises to them. Therefore, from the point of view of self-interest, we should keep our promises.

Pursuing this line of reasoning, Thomas Hobbes (1588–1679) suggested that the principle of Ethical Egoism leads to nothing less than the Golden Rule: We should "do unto others" so that others will be more likely to "do unto us."

Does this argument succeed in establishing Ethical Egoism as a viable theory of morality? It may be the best try. However, there are two serious problems with it. First, the argument does not prove as much as it needs to. It shows only that it is *usually* to one's advantage to tell the truth, to keep one's promises, and to avoid harming others. But a situation might arise in which you could profit from doing something horrible, like killing someone. In such a case, Ethical Egoism cannot explain why you shouldn't do the horrible thing. Thus, it looks like some of our moral obligations cannot be derived from self-interest.

Second, suppose that giving money to famine relief is somehow to one's own advantage. It doesn't follow that this is the *only* reason to do so. Another reason might be *to help the starving people.* Ethical Egoism says that self-interest is the only reason to help others, but nothing in the present argument really supports that.

5.4. Two Arguments against Ethical Egoism

The Argument That Ethical Egoism Endorses Wickedness. Consider these wicked actions, taken from various news stories: To make more money, a pharmacist filled prescriptions for cancer patients using watered-down drugs. A paramedic gave emergency patients injections of sterile water rather than morphine, so he could sell the morphine. Parents fed their baby acid, so they could fake a lawsuit, claiming the baby's formula was tainted. A male nurse raped two patients while they were unconscious. A 73-year-old man kept his daughter locked in a cellar for 24 years and fathered seven children with her, against her will. A 60-year-old man shot his letter carrier seven times because he was $90,000 in debt and thought that being in federal prison would be better than being homeless.

Suppose that someone could actually benefit from doing such things. Wouldn't Ethical Egoism have to approve of such actions? This seems like enough to discredit the doctrine. However, this objection might be unfair to Ethical Egoism, because in saying that these actions are wicked, it assumes a nonegoistic conception of wickedness.

The Argument That Ethical Egoism Is Unacceptably Arbitrary. This argument may refute Ethical Egoism. Unlike the previous argument, it tries to explain *why* the interests of other people should matter to us. But before examining it, let's consider a general point about moral values.

There is a family of moral views that have this in common: They divide people into groups and say that the interests of some groups count more than the interests of other groups. Racism is the most obvious example. Racists divide people into groups according to race and assign greater importance to the well-being of one race than to the well-being of other races. In fact, all forms of discrimination work like this—anti-Semitism, nationalism, sexism, and so on. People in the sway of such attitudes will think, in effect, "*My* race counts for more," or "People who believe in *my* religion count for more," or "*My* country counts for more," and so on.

Can such ideas be defended? The people who accept them don't usually give arguments for them—racists, for example, rarely try to justify racism. But suppose they did. What could they say?

There is a general principle that stands in the way of any such justification. Let's call it the Principle of Equal Treatment: *We should treat people in the same way unless there is a good reason not to.* For example, suppose we're considering whether to admit two students to law school. If both students graduated from college with honors and aced the entrance exam—if both are equally qualified—then it is arbitrary to admit one but not the other. However, if one graduated with honors and scored well on the admissions test while the other dropped out of college and never took the test, then it is acceptable to admit the first student but not the second.

At root, the Principle of Equal Treatment is a principle that requires fairness in our dealings with others: Like cases should be treated alike, and only dissimilar cases may be treated differently. Two points should be made about the principle. The first is that treating people in the same way does not always mean ensuring the same outcome for them. During the Vietnam War, young American men desperately wanted to avoid getting drafted into the armed services, and the government had to decide the order in which draft boards would call people up. In 1969, the first "draft lottery" was televised to a national audience. Here is how it worked: The days of the year were written on 366 slips of paper (one slip for February 29) and inserted into blue plastic capsules. Those capsules were placed in a glass jar and mixed up. Then, one by one, the capsules were drawn. September 14 was drawn first—so, young men with that birthday, age 18–26, would be drafted first. The winners of the lottery, drawn last, were born on June 8. These young men never got drafted. In college dormitories, groups of students watched the drawings live, and it was easy to tell whose birthday had just come up—whoever just groaned or swore. Obviously, the outcomes were different: In the end, some people got drafted, and others didn't. However, the process was fair. By giving everyone an equal chance in the lottery, the government treated everyone in the same way.

A second point concerns the *scope* of the principle, or which situations it applies to. Suppose you're not going to use your ticket to the big game, and so you give it to a friend. In doing so, you are treating your friend better than everyone else you could have given the ticket to. Does your action violate the Principle of Equal Treatment? Does it need justification? Moral philosophers disagree about this. Some of them think that the principle does not apply to cases like this. The principle applies only in "moral contexts," and what you should do with your ticket is not important enough to count as a "moral question." Others think that your action does require justification, and various justifications might be given. Your action might be justified by the nature of friendship; or by the fact that it would be impossible for you to hold a lottery at the last minute for all the ticketless fans; or by the fact that you own the ticket, and so you can do what you want with it. For our purposes, in assessing Ethical Egoism, it doesn't matter exactly how these questions are answered. It's enough that everyone accepts the principle, under one interpretation or another. Everyone believes in treating people similarly, unless the facts demand otherwise.

Consider an example. When Donald Trump kicked off his candidacy for president in 2015, he said of Mexicans immigrants: "They're bringing drugs. They're bringing crime. They're rapists." And Trump soon widened his attack: "It's coming from more than Mexico. It's coming from all over South and Latin America...." The first remark sounds like nationalism: People are divided into two groups, based on their country of origin, and the people in one group (the Mexicans) are to be treated worse than the people in the other group (the non-Mexicans). Trump's second remark sounds like racism: People are now divided into two racial groups, Latinos and non-Latinos (or, perhaps, people with brown skin and people without such skin), and our immigration policy should favor those in the second group.

Note, however, that Trump did not merely indicate a preference for some groups over others; he also tried to give a reason for this: that Mexican and Latino immigrants to America (or brown people in general) are a bunch of criminals. In fact, that claim is false; people in America actually commit more crimes *if they were born in America* than if they were not. Evidently, people who want to come to America, and who make the effort to do so, behave better once they are in America than people who were simply born there. Thus, Trump's "justification" of his stance on immigration fails. But notice what else is true: Even Donald Trump believes in the Principle of Equal Treatment. Trump could have just said, "Let's keep Latinos out" without saying why. However, he knew that he had to try to give a reason: He needed to offer some factual basis for denying Latinos entry to the United States, given that other people *are* let in. So, he called them drug-dealing rapists. Stereotypes exist because even racists know that they must explain *why* the people they hate deserve worse treatment than others.

Ethical Egoism also violates the Principle of Equal Treatment. It divides the world into two groups of people—one's self and everyone else—and urges us to favor the interests of those in the first group over the interests of those in the second group. But each of us can ask the following questions: What is the difference between me and everyone else that justifies placing myself in this special category? Am I more intelligent? Are my accomplishments greater? Do I enjoy life more? Are my needs and abilities different from the needs and abilities of others? In short, *what makes me so special?* Failing an answer, it turns out that Ethical Egoism is an arbitrary doctrine, in the same way that nationalism and racism are arbitrary. Each doctrine violates the Principle of Equal Treatment.

We should care about other people because their needs and desires are comparable to our own. Similar cases should be treated similarly. Consider, one last time, the starving children we could feed by giving up some of our luxuries. Why should we care about them? We care about ourselves, of course—if *we* were starving, then we would do almost anything to get food for ourselves. But what is the difference between us and them? Does hunger affect them any less? Are they less deserving than we are? If we can find no relevant difference between us and them, then we must admit that if our needs should be met, then so should theirs. This realization—that we are on a par with one another—is the deepest reason why our morality must recognize the needs of others. And that is why, ultimately, Ethical Egoism fails as a moral theory.

Notes on Sources

The statistics on childhood mortality are from unicef.org ("Child Survival/ Under-Five Mortality"), accessed on August 30, 2017.

Fifty inches of rain on Houston: Todd C. Frankel, Avi Selk, and David A Fahrenthold, "Residents Warned to 'Get Out or Die' as Harvey Unleashes New Waves of Punishing Rains and Flooding," *The Washington Post*, August 30, 2017.

On Raoul Wallenberg, see John Bierman, *The Righteous Gentile* (New York: Viking Press, 1981), and Sewell Chan, "71 Years after He Vanished, Raoul Wallenberg Is Declared Dead," *The New York Times*, October 31, 2016. On Gentiles who risked their lives to protect Jews, see http://www .yadvashem.org.

On Zell Kravinsky, see Ian Parker's "The Gift," in the *New Yorker* (August 2, 2004). On Oseola McCarty, see Bill Clinton, *Giving: How Each of Us Can Change the World* (New York: Alfred A. Knopf, 2007), p. 26.

Dale Carnegie, *How to Win Friends and Influence People* (New York: Simon and Schuster, 1981; first published in 1936), p. 31.

The story about Abraham Lincoln is from the Springfield *Monitor*, quoted by Frank Sharp in his *Ethics* (New York: Appleton Century, 1928), p. 75.

Cara Buckley, "Man Is Rescued by Stranger on Subway Tracks," *The New York Times* (January 3, 2007).

Ayn Rand is quoted from her book *The Virtue of Selfishness* (New York: Signet, 1964), pp. 27, 32, 80, and 81.

The newspaper stories are from *The Baltimore Sun*, August 28, 2001; *The Miami Herald*, August 28, 1993, October 6, 1994, and June 2, 1989; *The New York Times*, April 28, 2008; and the *Macon Telegraph*, July 15, 2005.

Donald Trump's June 16, 2015, speech can be read at "Here's Donald Trump's Presidential Announcement Speech" on time.com. Also see Richard Perez-Penajan, "Contrary to Trump's Claims, Immigrants Are Less Likely to Commit Crimes," *The New York Times*, January 26, 2017.

CHAPTER 6

T*he Social Contract Theory*

Wherever law ends, tyranny begins . . .
JOHN LOCKE, *THE SECOND TREATISE OF GOVERNMENT* (1690)

6.1. Hobbes's Argument

Suppose we take away all the traditional props for morality. Assume, first, that there is no God to issue commands and reward virtue. Next, suppose that there are no "natural purposes"—objects in nature have no inherent functions or intended uses. Finally, assume that human beings are naturally selfish. Where, then, could morality come from? If we cannot appeal to God, natural purpose, or altruism, is there anything left to base morality on?

Thomas Hobbes, the leading British philosopher of the 17th century, tried to show that morality does not depend on any of those things. Instead, morality should be understood as the solution to a practical problem that arises for self-interested human beings. We all want to live as well as possible; but in order to flourish, we need a peaceful, cooperative social order. And we cannot have one without rules. Those rules *are* the moral rules; morality consists of the precepts we need to follow in order to get the benefits of social living. That—not God, inherent purposes, or altruism—is the key to understanding ethics.

Hobbes begins by asking what it would be like if there were no way to enforce social rules. Suppose there were no government institutions—no laws, no police, and no courts. In this situation, each of us would be free to do as we pleased. Hobbes called this "the state of nature." What would it be like? Hobbes thought it would be dreadful. In the state of nature, he says, there would be no place for industry, because the fruit thereof is uncertain: and consequently no culture of the earth; no navigation, nor use of the commodities that may be imported by sea; no commodious building; no instruments of moving, and removing, such things as require much force; no knowledge of the face of the earth; no account of time; no arts; no letters; no society; and which is worst of all, continual fear, and danger of violent death; and the life of man, solitary, poor, nasty, brutish, and short.

The state of nature would be awful, Hobbes thought, due to four basic facts about human life:

- There is *equality of need*. Each of us needs the same basic things in order to survive—food, clothing, shelter, and so on. Although we differ in some of our needs (diabetics need insulin, others don't), we are all essentially alike.
- There is *scarcity*. We do not live in the Garden of Eden, where milk flows in streams and every tree hangs heavy with fruit. The world is a hard, inhospitable place, where the things we need do not come in abundance. We have to work hard to produce them, and even then they may be in short supply.
- There is *the essential equality of human power*. Who will get the scarce goods? No one can simply take what she wants. Even though some people are smarter and tougher than others, even the strongest can be brought down when those who are less strong act together.
- Finally, there is *limited altruism*. If we cannot prevail by our own strength, what hope do we have? Can we rely on the goodwill of others? We cannot. Even if people are not wholly selfish, they care most about themselves, and we cannot assume that they will step aside when their interests conflict with ours.

Together, these facts paint a grim picture. We all need the same basic things, and there aren't enough of them to go around. Therefore, we will have to compete for them. But no one can prevail in this competition, and no one—or almost no one—will look after his neighbors. The result, as Hobbes puts it, is a "constant state of war, of one with all." And it is a war no one can win. Whoever wants to survive will try to seize what he needs and prepare to defend it from attack. Meanwhile, others will be doing the same thing. Life in the state of nature would be intolerable.

Hobbes did not think that all this was mere speculation. He pointed out that this is what actually happens when governments collapse during civil uprisings. People hoard food, arm themselves, and lock out their neighbors. Moreover, nations themselves behave like this when international law is weak. Without a strong, overarching authority to maintain the peace, countries guard their borders, build up their armies, and feed their own people first.

To escape the state of nature, we must find a way to work together. In a stable and cooperative society, we can produce more essential goods and distribute them in a rational way. But establishing such a society is not easy. People must agree on rules to govern their interactions. They must agree, for example, not to harm one another and not to break their promises. Hobbes calls such an agreement "the social contract." As a society, we follow certain rules, and we have ways to enforce them. Some of those ways involve the law—if you assault someone, the police may arrest you. Other ways involve "the court of public opinion"—if you get a reputation for lying, then people may turn their backs on you. All of these rules, taken together, form the social contract.

It is only within the context of the social contract that we can become beneficent beings, because the contract creates the conditions under which we can afford to care about others. In the state of nature, it is every man for himself; it would be foolish for anyone to look out for others and put his own interests in jeopardy. But in society, altruism becomes possible. By releasing us from "the continual fear of violent death," the social contract frees us to take heed of others. Jean-Jacques Rousseau (1712–1778) went so far as to say that we become *different kinds of creatures* when we enter civilized relations with others. In *The Social Contract* (1762), he writes,

> The passage from the state of nature to the civil state produces
> a very remarkable change in man. . . . Then only, when the
> voice of duty takes the place of physical impulses . . . does man,
> who so far had considered only himself, find that he is forced

to act on different principles, and to consult his reason before listening to his inclinations. . . . His faculties are so stimulated and developed, . . . his feelings so ennobled, and his whole soul so uplifted, that, did not the abuses of this new condition often degrade him below that which he left, he would be bound to bless continually the happy moment which took him from it forever, and, instead of a stupid and unimaginative animal, made him an intelligent being and a man.

And what does the "voice of duty" require this new man to do? It requires him to set aside his self-centered designs in favor of rules that benefit everyone. But he is able to do this only because others have made the same pledge—that is the essence of the "contract."

The Social Contract Theory explains the purpose of both morality and government. The purpose of morality is to make social living possible; the purpose of government is to enforce vital moral rules. We can summarize the social contract conception of morality as follows: *Morality consists in the set of rules, governing behavior, that rational people will accept, on the condition that others accept them as well.* And rational people will accept a rule only if they can expect to gain from it. Thus, morality is about mutual benefit; you and I are morally bound to follow a rule only if we would be better off living in a society in which that rule was usually followed.

6.2. The Prisoner's Dilemma

Hobbes's argument is one way of arriving at the Social Contract Theory. Another argument makes use of the Prisoner's Dilemma—a problem invented by Merrill M. Flood and Melvin Dresher around 1950. Here's how the problem goes.

Suppose you live in a totalitarian society, and one day, to your astonishment, you are arrested and charged with treason. The police say that you have been plotting against the government with a man named Smith, who has also been arrested and is being held in a separate cell. The interrogator demands that you confess. You protest your innocence; you don't even know Smith. But this does you no good. It soon becomes clear that your captors are not interested ll the truth, they merely want to convict someone. They offer you the following deal:

- If Smith does not confess, but you confess and testify against him, then they will release you. You will go free, while Smith will be put away for 10 years.
- If Smith confesses and you do not, the situation will be reversed—he will go free while you get 10 years.
- If you both confess, you will each be sentenced to 5 years.
- If neither of you confesses, then there won't be enough evidence to convict either of you. They can hold you for a year, but then they will have to let both of you go.

Finally, you are told that Smith is being offered the same deal, but you cannot communicate with him, and you have no way of knowing what he will do.

The problem is this: Assuming that your only goal is to spend as little time in jail as possible, what should you do? Confess or not confess? For the purposes of this problem, you should forget about maintaining your dignity and standing up for your rights. That is not what this problem is about. You should also forget about trying to help Smith. This problem is strictly about calculating what is in your own best interests. What will get you free the quickest?

The question may seem impossible to answer unless you know what Smith will do. But that is an illusion. The problem has a clear solution: No matter what Smith does, you should confess. This can be shown as follows:

(1) Either Smith will confess or he won't.
(2) Suppose Smith confesses. Then, if you confess you will get 5 years, whereas if you do not confess you will get 10 years. Therefore, if he confesses, you are better off confessing.
(3) On the other hand, suppose Smith does not confess. Then, if you confess you will go free, whereas if you do not confess you get one year. Therefore, if Smith does not confess, you will still be better off confessing.
(4) Therefore, you should confess. That will get you out of jail the soonest, no matter what Smith does.

So far, so good. But remember that Smith is being offered the same deal. Thus, he will also confess. The result will be that you both get 5-year sentences. *But if you had both done the opposite, you both could have gotten only one year.* It's a curious situation: Because you and Smith both act selfishly, you both wind up worse off.

Now suppose you can communicate with Smith. In that case, you could make a deal with him. You could agree that neither of you will confess; then you will both get the one-year detention. By cooperating, you will both be better off than if you act independently. Cooperating will not get either of you the best result—immediate freedom—but it will get both of you a better result than you would have gotten alone.

It is vital, however, that any agreement between you and Smith be enforceable, because if he reneges and confesses while you keep the bargain, you will end up serving the maximum 10 years while he goes free. Thus, in order for you to rationally participate in such a deal, you need to be sure that Smith will keep up his end.

Morality as the Solution to Prisoner's-Dilemma-Type Problems. The Prisoner's Dilemma is not just a clever puzzle. Although the story it tells is fictitious, the pattern it exemplifies comes up often in real life. Consider, for example, the choice between two general strategies of living. You could pursue your own interests exclusively—in every situation, you could do whatever will benefit yourself, taking no notice of anyone else. Let us call this "acting selfishly." Alternatively, you could care about others, balancing their interests against your own and sometimes forgoing your own interests for their sake. Let us call this strategy "acting benevolently."

But it is not only you who must decide. Other people also have to choose which strategy to adopt. There are four possibilities: (a) You could be selfish while other people are benevolent; (b) others could be selfish while you are benevolent; (c) everyone could be selfish; and (d) everyone could be benevolent. How would you fare in each of these situations? You might assess the possibilities like this:

- You would be best off if you were selfish while other people were benevolent. You would get the benefit of their generosity without having to return the favor. (In this situation, you would be a "free rider.")

- Second-best would be if everyone were benevolent. You would no longer have the advantages that come from ignoring other people's interests, but you would be treated well by others. (This is the situation of "ordinary morality.")

- A bad situation, but not the worst, would be one in which everyone was selfish. You would try to protect your own interests, but you would get little help from others. (This is Hobbes's "state of nature.")

- You would be worst off if you were benevolent while others were selfish. Other people could stab you in the back whenever they wanted, but you would never do the same. You would come out on the short end every time. (This is the "sucker's payoff.")

This situation has the same structure as the Prisoner's Dilemma. In fact, it *is* a Prisoner's Dilemma, even though it involves no prisoners. Again, we can prove that you should adopt the selfish strategy:

(1) Either other people will respect your interests or they won't.

(2) If they do respect your interests, you would be better off not respecting theirs, at least when that would be to your benefit. This would be the optimum situation—you get to be a free rider.

(3) If they do not respect your interests, then it would be foolish for you to respect theirs. That would land you in the worst possible situation—you get the sucker's payoff.

(4) Therefore, regardless of what other people do, you are better off adopting the policy of looking out for yourself. You should be selfish.

And now we come to the catch: Other people, of course, can reason in this same way, and the result will be Hobbes's state of nature. Everyone will be selfish, willing to knife anyone who gets in their way. In that situation, each of us would be worse off than if we all cooperated.

To escape the dilemma, we need another enforceable agreement, this time to obey the rules of mutually respectful social living.

THE SOCIAL CONTRACT THEORY 91

As before, cooperation will not yield the optimum outcome for each individual, but it will lead to a better result than non-cooperation. We need, in David Gauthier's words, to "bargain our way into morality." We can do that by establishing laws and social customs that protect the interests of everyone involved.

6.3. Some Advantages of the Social Contract Theory

Morality, on this theory, consists in the rules that rational people will accept, on the condition that others accept them as well. The strength of this theory is due, in large part, to the fact that it provides plausible answers to some difficult questions.

1. *What moral rules are we bound to follow, and how are those rules justified?* The morally binding rules are the ones that facilitate harmonious social living. We could not live together in peace if we allowed murder, assault, theft, lying, promise breaking, and so on. The rules forbidding those acts are, therefore, justified by their tendency to promote harmony and cooperation. On the other hand, "moral rules" that condemn prostitution, sodomy, and sexual promiscuity cannot be justified on these grounds. How is social living hampered by private, voluntary sexual activity? How would it benefit us to agree to such rules? What people do behind closed doors is outside the scope of the social contract. Such rules, therefore, have no claim on us.

2. *Why is it rational for us to follow the moral rules?* We *agree* to follow the moral rules because we benefit from living in a place where the rules are accepted. However, we *actually do* follow the rules—we keep our end of the bargain—because the rules will be enforced, and it is rational for us to avoid punishment. Why don't you kidnap your boss? Because you might get caught.

But what if you think you won't get caught? Why follow the rules then? To answer this question, first note that you don't want *other* people to break the rules when they think they can avoid punishment—you don't want other people to commit murder, assault, and so on, just because they think they can get away with it. After all, they might be murdering or assaulting *you*. For this reason, we want others to accept the contract in more than a frivolous or light-hearted way. We want them to form a *firm intention* to hold up their end of the bargain; we want them to become the sort of people who won't be tempted to stray. And, of course, they will demand the same of us, as part of the agreement. But once we have this firm intention, it is rational to act on it. Why don't you kidnap your boss when you think you can get away with it? Because you've made a firm decision not to be that sort of person.

3. *Under what circumstances is it rational to break the rules?* We agree to obey the rules only on certain conditions. One condition is that we benefit from the overall arrangement. Another condition is that other people will do their part. Thus, when someone breaks the rules, he releases us from our obligations toward him. For example, suppose someone refuses to help you in circumstances in which he clearly should. If later on he needs your help, you may rightly feel that you have no duty to help him.

The same point explains why punishing criminals is acceptable. Lawbreakers are treated differently from other citizens—in punishing them, we treat them in ways that are normally forbidden, ways that they themselves wouldn't agree to. Why can we do this? Remember that the rules apply to you only if other people also follow them. So, you may disregard those rules when dealing with someone who doesn't follow them. In breaking the rules, the criminal thus leaves himself open to retaliation. This explains why it is legitimate for the government to enforce the law.

4. *How much can morality demand of us?* Morality seems to require that we be impartial—that is, that we give no greater weight to our own interests than to the interests of others. But suppose you face a situation in which you must choose between your own death and the deaths of five other people. Impartiality, it seems, would require you to choose your own death; after all, there are five of them and only one of you. Are you morally bound to sacrifice yourself?

Philosophers have often felt uneasy about this sort of example; they have felt instinctively that there are limits to what morality can demand of us. Therefore, they have traditionally said that such heroic actions are *supererogatory*—that is, above and beyond the call of duty, admirable when they occur but not morally required. Yet it is hard to explain why such actions are not required. If morality demands impartial behavior, and it is better that one person die rather than five, then you should be required to sacrifice yourself.

What does the Social Contract Theory say about this? Suppose the question is whether to have the rule "If you can save many lives by sacrificing your own life, then you must do so." Would it be rational to accept this rule, on the condition that everyone else accepts it? Presumably, it would be. After all, each of us is more likely to benefit from this rule than to be harmed by it—you're more likely to be among those saved than to be the one and only person who gives up her life. Thus, it may seem that the Social Contract Theory does require moral heroism.

But this is not so. On the Social Contract Theory, morality consists in the rules that rational people will accept *on the condition that others accept them as well.* However, it would not be rational to make an agreement that we don't expect others to follow. Can we expect other people to follow this rule of self-sacrifice—can we expect strangers to form a firm intention to give up their lives for us? We cannot. Most people won't be that benevolent, even if they have promised to be. Can we expect the threat of punishment to *make them* that benevolent? Again, we cannot; people's fear of death is likely to overwhelm any fear they have of punishment. Thus, there is a natural limit to the amount of self-sacrifice that the social contract can require: Rational people will not agree to rules so demanding that others won't follow them. In this way, the Social Contract Theory explains a feature of morality that other theories find mysterious.

6.4. The Problem of Civil Disobedience

Moral theories should help us understand concrete moral issues. The Social Contract Theory in particular should help us understand issues about social institutions—after all, explaining the proper function of those institutions is one of the main goals of the theory. So let's consider again our obligation to obey the law. Are we ever justified in breaking the law? If so, when?

Civil disobedience is a form of nonviolent protest against the government, where people break the law openly and do not resist arrest. The great modern examples of it are from the Indian independence movement, led by Mohandas K. Gandhi (1869-1948), and the American civil rights movement, led by Martin Luther King Jr. (1929-1968). Both movements were characterized by public, conscientious, nonviolent refusal to comply with the law. In 1930, Gandhi and his followers marched to the coastal village of Dandi, where they defied British law by distilling salt from saltwater. The British had been controlling salt production in order to force the Indian peasants to buy it at high prices. In America, Dr. King led the Montgomery Bus Boycott, which began in Alabama's capital after Rosa Parks was arrested on December 1, 1955, for refusing to give up her bus seat to a white man. Parks was defying one of the "Jim Crow" laws designed to enforce racial segregation in the South. Gandhi and King, the two greatest proponents of nonviolence in the 20th century, were both murdered by gunfire.

Their movements had different goals. Gandhi and his followers did not recognize the right of the British to govern India; they wanted to replace British rule with self-governance. King and his followers, however, did not question the legitimacy of the American government. They objected only to particular laws and particular social policies. For most of the 20th century, people of color were treated as an inferior underclass in America, especially in the South. In the South, places such as schools, restaurants, water fountains, bathrooms, and pools were segregated by race, and the "colored facilities" were always rundown as compared to the places where white people were welcome. African-Americans were poor, and a century after slavery, neighborhoods across America remained highly segregated, due to racist practices in the housing market. In the South, few African-Americans could vote because most municipalities made it impossible for them to register. In addition, blacks could not expect fair treatment from the legal system, where every police officer, judge, and juror was white.

Racial segregation was not only enforced by social custom, but it was also a matter of *law*, of laws that black citizens were denied a voice in formulating. When urged to rely on ordinary democratic processes, King pointed out that all attempts to use these processes had failed. And as for "democracy," he said, that word has no meaning for those who have been denied the right to vote. Hence, King believed that blacks had no choice but to defy the unjust laws and to accept the consequences by going to jail.

Today we remember King as a great moral leader. At the time, however, his strategy of civil disobedience was highly controversial. Many liberals expressed sympathy for his goals but criticized his tactic of breaking the law. An article in the *New York State Bar Journal* in 1965 expressed the typical worries. After assuring his readers that "long before Dr. King was born, I espoused, and still espouse, the cause of civil rights for all people," Louis Waldman, a prominent New York lawyer, argues,

> Those who assert rights under the Constitution and the laws made thereunder must abide by that Constitution and the law, if that Constitution is to survive. They cannot pick and choose; they cannot say they will abide by those laws which they think are just and refuse to abide by those laws which they think are unjust. . . .
>
> The country, therefore, cannot accept Dr. King's doctrine that he and his followers will pick and choose, knowing that it is illegal to do so. I say, such doctrine is not only illegal and for that reason alone should be abandoned, but that it is also immoral, destructive of the principles of democratic government, and a danger to the very civil rights Dr. King seeks to promote.

Waldman had a point: If our legal system is basically decent, then defying the law is, on its face, a bad thing because it might weaken people's respect for the law generally. To meet this objection, King sometimes said that the evils he opposed were so serious, so numerous, and so difficult to fight that civil disobedience was justified as a last resort. The end justifies the means, though the means are imperfect. This argument may be enough to answer Waldman's objections. But there is a more profound reply available.

According to the Social Contract Theory, we are obligated to obey the law because we each participate in a social system that promises more benefits than burdens. The benefits are the benefits of social living: We escape the state of nature and live in a society in which we are secure and enjoy basic rights. To gain these benefits, we agree to uphold the institutions that make them possible. This means that we must obey the law, pay our taxes, serve on juries, and so forth—these are the burdens we accept in return.

But what if some citizens are denied their basic rights? What if the police, instead of protecting those citizens, attack them with dogs while protecting those who lynch them? Under such circumstances, the social contract is not being honored. In asking the disadvantaged group to obey the law and pay their taxes and respect society's institutions, we are asking them to accept the burdens of social living without receiving its benefits.

This line of reasoning suggests that civil disobedience is not an undesirable "last resort" for socially disenfranchised groups. Rather, it is the most natural and reasonable means of expressing protest. For when the disadvantaged are denied the benefits of social living, they are released from the contract that would otherwise require them to follow society's rules. This is the deepest argument for civil disobedience, and the Social Contract Theory presents it clearly and forcefully.

6.5. Difficulties for the Theory

The Social Contract Theory is one of the major options in contemporary moral philosophy, along with Utilitarianism, Kantianism, and Virtue Ethics. It is easy to see why; the theory seems to explain a great deal about moral life. Two important objections, however, have been made against it.

First, it is said that the Social Contract Theory is based on a historical fiction. We are asked to imagine that people once lived in isolation from one another, that they found this intolerable, and that they eventually banded together, agreeing to follow social rules of mutual benefit. But none of this ever happened. It is just a fantasy. So of what relevance is it? To be sure, if people *had* come together in this way, we could explain their obligations to one another as the theory suggests: They would be obligated to obey the rules that they had agreed to obey. But even then, there would be problems. Was the agreement unanimous? If not, what about the people who didn't sign up—are they *not* required to act morally? And if the contract was made a long time ago by our ancestors, why should *we* be bound to it? But anyway, there never was such a contract, and so nothing can be explained by appealing to it. As one critic wisecracked, the social contract "isn't worth the paper it's not written on."

To be sure, none of us ever signed a "real" contract—there is no piece of paper bearing our signatures. Immigrants, who promise to obey the law when they are granted citizenship, are the exception. The contract theorist might say, however, that a social arrangement like the one described does exist, for all of us: There is a set of rules that everyone recognizes as binding on them, and we all benefit from the fact that these rules are generally followed. Each of us accepts the benefits conferred by this arrangement; and, more than that, we expect and encourage others to observe the rules. This describes the actual world; it is not fictitious. And, by accepting the benefits of this arrangement, we incur an obligation to do our part—which at least means that we should follow the rules. We are thus bound by an *implicit* social contract. It is "implicit" because we become a party to it, not by explicitly making a promise, but by accepting the benefits of social living.

Thus, the story of the "social contract" need not be intended as a description of historical events. Rather, it is a useful analytical tool, based on the idea that we may understand our moral obligations *as if* they had arisen in this way. Consider the following analogy: Suppose you come upon a group of people playing an elaborate game. It looks like fun, and you join in. After a while, however, you begin to break some of the rules, because that looks like more fun. When the other players protest, you say that you never promised to follow the rules. However, your remark is irrelevant. Perhaps nobody promised to obey, but, by joining the game, each person implicitly agreed to abide by the rules that make the game possible. It is *as though* they had all agreed. Morality is like this. The "game" is social living; the rules, which make the game possible, are the rules of morality.

That response to the first objection, however, is ineffective. When a game is in progress, and you join in, it is obvious that you *choose* to join in, because you could have just walked away. For that reason, you must respect the game's rules, or you will rightly be regarded as a nuisance. By contrast, somebody born into today's big cooperative world does not *choose* to join it; nobody chooses to be born. And then, once a person has grown up, the costs of leaving that world are severe. How could you opt out? You might become a survivalist and never use electricity, roads, the water service, and so on. But that would be a great burden. Alternatively, you might leave the country. But what if you don't like the social rules that exist in any of the other countries, either? Moreover, as David Hume (1711–1776) observed, many people are not "free to leave their country" in any meaningful sense:

> Can we seriously say that a poor peasant . . . has a free choice to leave his country, when he knows no foreign language or manners, and lives from day to day by the small wages which he acquires? We may as well assert that a man, by remaining [on a ship], freely consents to the dominion of the master, though he was carried on board while asleep, and must leap into the ocean and perish the moment he leaves.

Thus, life is not like joining a game, whose rules you may reject by walking away. Rather, life is like being thrust into a game you can't walk away from. The contract theorist has not explained why one must obey the rules of such a game.

Does the first objection, therefore, refute the Social Contract Theory? I don't think so. The contract theorist may say this: Participating in a sensible social scheme is rational; it really is in one's best interest. *This is why the rules are valid*—because they benefit those who live under them. If someone doesn't agree to the rules, the rules still apply to him; he's just being irrational. Suppose, for example, that a survivalist forgoes the benefits of social living. May he then refuse to pay his taxes? He may not, because even he would be better off paying his taxes *and* enjoying the benefits of clean water, paved roads, indoor plumbing, and so on. The survivalist might not want to play the game, but the rules still apply to him, because it would really and truly be in his interest to join in.

This defense of the Social Contract Theory abandons the idea that morality is based on an agreement. However, it holds fast to the idea that morality consists in mutually beneficial rules. It also complies with our earlier definition, that *morality consists in the set of rules, governing behavior, that rational people will accept, on the condition that others accept them as well.* Rational people will accept rules of mutual benefit.

The second objection is more troubling. Some individuals cannot benefit us. Thus, according to the Social Contract Theory, these individuals have no claim on us; we may ignore their interests when we're writing up the "mutually beneficial" rules of society. The moral rules will, therefore, let us treat these individuals in any way whatsoever. This implication of the theory is unacceptable.

There would be at least three vulnerable groups:

• Nonhuman animals
• Future generations
• Oppressed populations

Suppose, for example, that a sadist wanted to torment a cat. *He* would not benefit from a system of rules forbidding the torture of cats; after all, he is not a cat, and he wants to be cruel. So, any rules forbidding feline cruelty would not apply to him. Of course, the cat's *owners* would be harmed under such a system—because they care about their cat—and so they might object to a system of rules allowing the torture of cats. In such cases, it is hard to know what moral rules would be valid. But suppose the sadist found some stray cats out in the woods. Now the Social Contract Theory cannot condemn him even if he commits acts of the greatest cruelty.

Or consider future generations. They cannot benefit us; we'll be dead before they are even born. Yet we can profit at their expense. Why shouldn't we run up the national debt? Why shouldn't we pollute the lakes and coat the skies with carbon dioxide? Why shouldn't we bury toxic waste in containers that will fall apart in a hundred years? It would not be against *our* interests to allow such actions; it would only harm our descendants. So, we may do so. Or consider oppressed populations. When the Europeans colonized new lands, why weren't they morally allowed to enslave the native inhabitants? After all, the native inhabitants did not have the weapons to put up a good fight. The Europeans could benefit most by creating a society in which the native inhabitants would be their slaves.

This type of objection does not concern some minor aspect of the theory; it goes right to the root of the tree. The Social Contract Theory is grounded in self-interest and reciprocity; thus, it seems unable to adequately recognize the moral duties we have to individuals who cannot benefit us.

Notes on Sources

The chapter-opening quote is from chapter 18, section 202, of Locke's *Second Treatise*. The full sentence reveals a different meaning than the partial passage: "Wherever law ends, tyranny begins if the law be transgressed to another's harm."

Hobbes on the state of nature: *Leviathan*, Oakeshott edition (Oxford: Blackwell, 1960), chapter 13 (see p. 82).

Rousseau is quoted from *The Social Contract and Discourses*, translated by G. D. H. Cole (New York: Dutton, 1959), pp. 18-19.

Flood and Dresher first formulated the Prisoner's Dilemma: Richmond Campbell, "Background for the Uninitiated," *Paradoxes of Rationality and Cooperation*, edited by Richmond Campbell and Lanning Sowden (Vancouver: University of British Columbia Press, 1985), p. 3.

On the experience of blacks in 20th-century America, including their treatment in housing, see Ta-Nehisi Coates, "The Case for Reparations," *The Atlantic*, June 2014.

On Louis Waldman, see *Civil Disobedience: Theory and Practice*, edited by Hugo Adam Bedau (New York: Pegasus Books, 1967), pp. 76-78 and 106-107.

David Hume, "Of the Original Contract," reprinted in *Hume's Moral and Political Philosophy*, edited by Henry D. Aiken (New York: Hafner, 1948), p. 363.

The Utilitarian Approach

The greatest happiness of the greatest number is the foundation of morals and legislation.

JEREMY BENTHAM, *COLLECTED WORKS* (1843)

7.1. The Revolution in Ethics

The late-18th and 19th centuries brought an astonishing series of upheavals: The modern nation-state emerged from the French Revolution (1787–1799) and the wreckage of the Napoleonic Empire (1804–1815); the revolutions of 1848 showed the power of "liberty, equality, and fraternity" as moral ideas; in the New World, America gained its independence from the British Empire and ratified a constitution promising an open and democratic society; and the American Civil War (1861–1865) finally ended the widespread use of slavery in Western civilization. All the while, the Industrial Revolution was reshaping the economies of the richest nations.

It is not surprising that new ideas about ethics emerged in this era. In particular, Jeremy Bentham (1748–1832) made a powerful argument for a novel conception of morality. Morality, he urged, is not about pleasing God, nor is it about being faithful to abstract rules; instead, it is about making the world as happy as possible. Bentham believed in one ultimate moral principle, the "Principle of Utility." That principle requires us, in all circumstances, to "maximize happiness"—in other words, to produce the greatest total balance of happiness over unhappiness, or of pleasure over suffering.

Bentham led a group of radicals who worked to reform the laws and institutions of England along utilitarian lines. One of his followers was James Mill, the distinguished Scottish philosopher, historian, and economist. James Mill's son, John Stuart Mill (1806-1873), would become the next leading advocate of utilitarian ethics. The younger Mill's advocacy was even more elegant and persuasive than Bentham's. Mill's short book *Utilitarianism* (1861) is still required reading for serious students of moral philosophy.

At first glance, the Principle of Utility might not seem so radical; in fact, it might seem trite or clichéd. After all, who *doesn't* believe that we should oppose suffering and promote happiness? Yet Bentham and Mill, in their own way, were as revolutionary as the two most celebrated intellectual innovators of the 19th century: the biologist Charles Darwin (1809-1882) and the social theorist Karl Marx (1818-1883).

To understand why the Principle of Utility was so radical, consider what it *leaves out* of morality: It says nothing about God, nor does it speak of abstract rules "written in the heavens." Morality is *not* viewed as obedience to a list of ancient proclamations. Or as the utilitarian Peter Singer (1946-) puts it, morality is not "a system of nasty puritanical prohibitions . . . designed to stop people [from] having fun." Rather, ethics is about the happiness of beings in this world, and nothing more; and we are permitted—even required—to do what is necessary to bring about the most happiness. This was no quaint truism; this was a revolutionary idea.

The utilitarians wanted their doctrine to matter in practice. So let's see what Utilitarianism has to say about three real-world issues: euthanasia, marijuana, and the treatment of nonhuman animals. This will give us a better sense of the theory.

7.2. First Example: Euthanasia

Sigmund Freud (1856-1939), the legendary Austrian psychologist, was stricken with oral cancer after decades of cigar smoking. During his final years, Freud's health went up and down, but in early 1939, a large swelling formed in the back of his mouth, and he would have no more good days. Freud's cancer was active, and he was also suffering from heart failure. As his bones decayed, they cast off a foul smell, driving away his favorite dog. Mosquito netting was draped over his bed in order to keep flies away.

On September 21, at the age of 83, Freud took his friend and personal physician, Max Schur, by the hand and said, "My dear

Schur, you certainly remember our first talk. You promised me then not to forsake me when my time comes. Now it's nothing but torture and makes no sense any more." Forty years earlier Freud had written, "What has the individual come to . . . if one no longer dares to disclose that it is this or that man's turn to die?" Dr. Schur said he understood. He injected Freud with a drug in order to end his life. "He soon felt relief," Dr. Schur wrote, "and fell into a peaceful sleep."

Did Max Schur do anything wrong? On the one hand, he had noble motives—he loved his friend and wanted to relieve his patient's misery. Moreover, Freud had asked to die. Those facts argue for a lenient judgment. On the other hand, what Schur did was morally wrong according to the dominant moral tradition in our culture.

That tradition is Christianity. Christianity holds that human life is a gift from God, and only God may decide to end it. The early church condemned all killing, believing that Jesus's teachings permitted no exceptions to the rule. Later, the church recognized some exceptions, such as capital punishment and killing in war. Suicide and euthanasia, however, remained forbidden. To summarize the church's doctrine, theologians formulated the rule: *The intentional killing of innocent human beings is always wrong.* This idea has shaped Western attitudes about the morality of killing. Thus, we may be reluctant to excuse Max Schur, despite his noble motives. He intentionally killed an innocent person; therefore, according to our tradition, what he did was wrong.

Utilitarianism sees things differently. It asks: Which action available to Max Schur would have produced the greatest balance of happiness over unhappiness? The person whose happiness was most at stake—by far—was Sigmund Freud. If Schur had not killed him, Freud would have lived on, in wretched pain. How much unhappiness would this have involved? It is hard to say precisely, but Freud strongly preferred death. Under such circumstances, utilitarians support the intentional killing of an innocent human being.

The utilitarian approach is secular, but Bentham denied that it goes against religion. Bentham even said that pious folks would *endorse* the utilitarian standpoint if only they (really and truly) viewed God as benevolent. He writes,

> The dictates of religion would coincide, in all cases, with those of utility, were the Being, who is the object of religion, universally supposed to be as benevolent as he is supposed to be wise and powerful. . . . But among the [advocates] of religion . . . there seem to be but few . . . who are real believers in his benevolence. They call him benevolent in words, but they do not mean that he is so in reality.

Mercy-killing might be a case in point. How, Bentham might ask, could a benevolent God forbid the killing of Sigmund Freud? If someone said, "God is caring and loving, but He forbids us from ending Freud's agony," this would be what Bentham means by "calling [God] benevolent in words, but not meaning that he is so in reality."

Most religious leaders, however, disagree with Bentham, and our legal tradition has been heavily influenced by Christianity. Among Western nations, euthanasia is legal in only a handful of countries. In the United States, it is simply murder, and a doctor who intentionally kills a patient could spend decades in prison. What would Utilitarianism say about this? If euthanasia is moral, on the utilitarian view, should it also be legal?

In general, if an action isn't wrong, then it should be allowed. Thus, mercy-killing should be allowed by law; it should be legal. Bentham believed that people should be free to do whatever they want—whatever they think will make them happy—so long as they aren't harming others. He opposed, for example, laws regulating the sexual conduct of consenting adults. Mill put this point eloquently in his book *On Liberty* (1859):

> The only purpose for which power can be rightfully exercised over any member of a civilized community, against his will, is to prevent harm to others. His own good, either physical or moral, is not a sufficient warrant. . . . Over himself, over his own body and mind, the individual is sovereign.

Hence, utilitarians see laws against euthanasia as restricting people's freedom, for no good reason. When Dr. Schur killed Freud, he was ending Freud's life in the manner that Freud had chosen. No one else was affected, and so it was no one else's business. Bentham himself is said to have requested euthanasia in his final days. However, we do not know if he died in the manner of Freud.

7.3. Second Example: Marijuana

The War on Drugs. On June 17, 1971, President Richard Nixon declared that drug abuse was "public enemy number one" in the United States. "In order to fight and defeat this enemy," Nixon said, "it is necessary to wage a new, all-out offensive." Thus began America's "War on Drugs." Since then, each president has waged that war with vigor, uniting with Congress to spend billions of dollars on law enforcement, prison construction, military action, and public-opinion campaigns, all designed to reduce the use of illicit drugs. And every state government joined in. Today, almost half a million people are prisoners of America's Drug War; roughly 20% of people incarcerated in the United States are locked up primarily due to nonviolent drug offenses.

Despite its name, the War on Drugs targets only some drugs. Many drugs are perfectly legal. Anyone can buy over-the-counter medications, which contain such drugs as aspirin. Also legal are three drugs that millions of Americans are addicted to: alcohol, caffeine, and nicotine.

Drugs that the Drug War *does* target are divided into five categories. Those categories, or "schedules," were defined in the Controlled Substances Act, a federal law that Nixon signed. According to that law, "Schedule One" drugs are the worst. Those drugs are considered so dangerous that, not only are they outlawed for personal use, but doctors cannot even prescribe them to patients. If drug abuse is public enemy number one, as Nixon said, then Schedule One Drugs must be the worst villains of all.

Among those villains is marijuana. The Controlled Substances Act has always classified marijuana as a Schedule One Drug. Thus, under federal law, *nobody* in the United States may grow, possess, or distribute cannabis, including doctors and pharmacists. In 2010, before any state had legalized weed, *most* drug arrests in the United States were for marijuana, and most of those arrests were for simple possession. Marijuana, it seems, has been the main enemy in the War on Drugs.

Growing Support for Marijuana Reform. During the past fifty years, many Americans have opposed the Drug War, at least in their private behavior, from time to time: marijuana has always been popular.

A recent poll found that 52% of adults have tried marijuana, and 22% are current users. For such reasons, perhaps, the drug has many nicknames. A federal-government website notes that marijuana is sometimes called "pot," "weed," "bud," "herb," "grass," "ganja," and "Mary Jane"—to which we may add "reefer," "chronic," "cannabis," "dope," "schwag," "skunk," "stinkweed," "gangster," "420," "THC," and "the Devil's lettuce." Yet most Americans—Democrats and Republicans alike—have supported the War on Drugs, ever since Nixon declared it.

In the last decade, however, many states have passed pro-marijuana laws in defiance of the Controlled Substances Act. By 2018, most states had legalized marijuana for medical purposes (for example, for treating nausea in cancer patients), while eight states, including California, had legalized it outright. Today, more than 20% of Americans live in states with laws that let adults purchase pot in certain places, just as adults might buy vodka at a package store or liquor store.

What happens, in practice, when a state law conflicts with a federal law? Usually, the state law is deemed null and void, because the U.S. Constitution says that federal laws get priority. In this case, however, the federal government has decided—so far—not to enforce the Controlled Substances Act against people who use weed in states that have legalized it. Given the nature of politics, perhaps that's unsurprising; a recent poll of Americans found broad support for the reform of marijuana laws, with 61% supporting full legalization, 88% in favor of medical marijuana, and 71% wanting the federal government to let states do as they wish.

The Pros and Cons of Marijuana Use. For utilitarians, the morality of pot depends solely on how pot affects people's happiness. Yet the issues lurking here are complex: Millions of people are affected in different ways by whether marijuana is legal, and even the smaller question of whether some particular person should use the drug on some particular occasion seems to invite a variety of responses. How, then, can a utilitarian expect to reach any firm conclusions about the overall happiness?

There are no guarantees, but when an issue is complex, utilitarians will often assess a proposed course of action by listing its pros and cons, where the "pros" are the ways in which it might increase happiness, and the "cons" are the ways in which it might decrease happiness. Then, once everything is laid out, one can try to judge the balance of those factors. So let's apply this method to two questions about pot. One concerns the law: Should marijuana be legal? The other question, which we'll consider first, concerns the well-being of individuals: how does getting high affect people's happiness? In other words, what are the harms and benefits of using weed?

The main benefit is pleasure. Marijuana is enormously relaxing, and it can greatly enhance the pleasure of sensory activities, such as eating, listening to music, and having sex. That fact is not always mentioned in public debates; sometimes, people seem to assume that enjoyment is irrelevant to ethics. Utilitarians, however, disagree. For them, enjoyment is central to ethics. Utilitarians value pleasure, and they do not believe that pleasures obtained through drugs are inherently worse than other pleasures. Utilitarians do not believe in "evil pleasures"—that is, in pleasures that are bad by their very nature. If something feels good, then it is good, at least to that extent. Being high feels good to a lot of people, and their pleasure matters as much as anyone else's.

What harm does marijuana do? Some of the charges made against it are untrue. First, almost one-fourth of Americans believe that marijuana leads to violence. Yet the opposite is true: Being high makes people calm and passive, not angry and aggressive. Second, marijuana has been said to be highly addictive. Yet experts believe that it is less addictive than either caffeine or alcohol. Third, pot has been called a "gateway drug" that leads people to "experiment with" harder, and presumably more dangerous, drugs. And that claim might be supported with the observation that heroin addicts usually tried pot first. In response, however, marijuana does not cause a craving for other drugs. Instead, it causes a craving for food—"the munchies." And while marijuana *is* typically tried before heroin, that fact is unsurprising, given that marijuana is more widely available. To make an analogy: Almost every cocaine addict first tried caffeine, but that fact is no indication that Coke is a gateway to coke.

Yet marijuana does have drawbacks. First, even if it's not *highly* addictive, some people become dependent on it and will withdraw if they stop using it. The withdrawal process isn't horrible—it isn't like heroin or nicotine withdrawal—but it can be unpleasant for several days. Second, marijuana can produce paranoia, especially if one gets high in a socially uncomfortable environment (or in a place where someone might suddenly knock on the door). Third, extended heavy use tends to make people less sharp, mentally. Note, however, that utilitarians might disagree about whether losing a little brainpower makes people less happy. Fourth, heavy users sometimes fall into a lethargy that makes them both unproductive and undependable—which not only harms them but also harms those who depend on them, such as roommates and family members.

Heavy use also increases one's chances of getting two terrible diseases: testicular cancer, which can be fatal, and schizophrenia, a long-term mental disorder. The risk of schizophrenia is greatest to young users, because schizophrenia tends to strike young adults. The extent of both of those risks, however, may be unclear; we know less about marijuana than about, say, tobacco. Yet our evidence strongly suggests that heavy pot-smoking is bad for one's respiratory system and gums. Note, however, that this might be because the pot is *smoked*. No studies have shown that consuming cannabis in other ways—for example, in pills or brownies—harms one's gums or one's ability to breathe.

What should we conclude about marijuana use? When we consider the harms and benefits, *occasional* use hardly even seems like a moral issue; the biggest risk it carries is the risk of getting arrested. Thus, utilitarians consider casual use to be a matter of personal preference and, where pot is illegal, of being careful so as not to get caught.

Heavy use is harder to assess. For people who enjoy marijuana, does their enhanced pleasure and reduced stress outweigh the risks of lethargy and disease—including the toll that their lethargy might take on others? One thought is that, to make a full comparison of the harms and benefits, we should also consider the health *benefits* that might come from leading a less stressful life. At any rate, utilitarians are free to disagree about whether using pot heavily is a good idea.

The Pros and Cons of Marijuana Legalization. What about the law—should utilitarians want pot to be legal? Most of the harms of legalization have already been discussed: an increased risk of certain diseases, more paranoia, more lethargy, and less productivity. The only other harm to consider is traffic accidents. Currently, however, the studies disagree about whether car crashes occur more often when drivers are high. This is because there's a trade-off: On the one hand, stoned drivers are easily distracted and may react slowly to unexpected dangers; yet potheads also drive defensively and are especially aware of their surroundings, because marijuana heightens the senses. Thus, a typical stoned driver is acutely aware yet easily distracted, and may react slowly to trouble yet may encounter less of it, due to his or her cautious driving-habits.

What are the *benefits* of legalizing marijuana? A benefit already discussed is the pleasure of the users. According to Utilitarianism, not only is pleasure a reason for you to get high, it is also a reason to let others get high—in other words, to support legal weed.

A second benefit is that users would no longer get arrested and imprisoned. In 2015, there were over 570,000 arrests for marijuana possession—more than were made for all violent crimes *combined*. Not only is being arrested and locked up awful, but ex-convicts have a hard time finding decent jobs, and even people who are arrested but never prosecuted can be charged a fee by the police station. Utilitarians care about every harm, even the harms that are inflicted on lawbreakers who knew they might get caught.

A third benefit is economic. Where marijuana is illegal, society spends money on enforcing the law; where marijuana is legal, society makes money by taxing the drug. For example, Colorado collected an extra $2 million in taxes during its first *month* of legal marijuana sales. And in 2015, Colorado's marijuana industry created more than 18,000 full-time jobs and generated almost $2.4 billion in economic activity, some of it from "marijuana tourists"—people who visited Colorado primarily to get high.

A fourth benefit is improved relations between minority communities and police. In the early 1970s, the "Jim Crow" era of legally enforced racial segregation in the United States was ending. Yet many people of color experienced the Drug War as a continuation of Jim Crow: The brutal enforcement of racism had merely been replaced by a zealous quest to arrest and imprison nonviolent African-American men. A recent study found that, among

Americans who use pot, blacks are *over four times* more likely than whites to be arrested for possession. The War on Drugs has thus generated great resentment in minority communities. This resentment is not only bad in itself, but it has also hindered the police in many of their efforts to catch *violent* criminals. For when a violent crime occurs in a minority neighborhood, residents at the scene are often reluctant to help investigating officers, because they see the police as their enemy—as the people who break down doors in the middle of the night in order to put somebody's nonviolent father, son, or brother in a locked cage. Legalization could improve community relations.

A fifth benefit is less drug violence around the world, especially in Latin America. For decades, the United States has pressured its neighbors to participate in its Drug War. And many of them have; they have tried to crack down on the making and moving of drugs within their own borders. Yet their efforts have often encountered fierce internal resistance, especially when people doing well in the drug business would become poor if they had to find other work. Thus, government forces often wind up fighting private armies whose soldiers are well-financed by drugs and well-motivated by their desire to have a decent quality of life. In Mexico, such conflicts have turned into a long, bloody war between various law-enforcement agencies and various criminal organizations. Legalizing marijuana would not solve all of these problems, but it would help.

A sixth benefit is that if people use more pot, then they might use other, more harmful drugs less. Of course, this won't be true of everyone. Some people might use more marijuana, without cutting back on any other drugs. Most people, however, will use other drugs less, for two reasons. First, pot might give them a better version of whatever benefit they were getting from the other drug. Hence, they might *replace* the other drug, at least to some extent, with marijuana. Consider, for example, alcohol. People who drink vodka in order to unwind, fall asleep, or ease their pain, might find marijuana more effective in these regards. So, they might drink less. The second reason is financial: One drug is cheaper than two. A pile of weed costs less than a pile of weed *plus* a bottle of rum. Hence, some people who use more weed will drink less rum.

Would society benefit if marijuana replaced alcohol as the main recreational drug? Indeed it would. Although marijuana doesn't cause violence, alcohol does; many people become angry and abusive when they get drunk. Alcohol also impairs driving *severely*. Moreover, heavy drinking leads to an unpleasant hangover, which can cause the drinker to be as unproductive as the marijuana user. And again, the economic costs of alcohol abuse are huge. In 2010, the total cost to Americans—which includes medical bills, lost wages, legal fees, and funeral expenses—has been estimated at a staggering $249 billion. Finally, and most importantly, alcohol causes more deaths: You can't overdose on marijuana, but you can die from acute alcohol poisoning. Alcohol kills around 88,000 Americans per year, mainly through liver disease, fetal alcohol syndrome, strokes, and car accidents. The victims of alcohol die, on average, about 30 years prematurely; alcohol kills young and old alike.

Legalization would also save lives by reducing the deadly abuse of opioid narcotics. The opioids include morphine, heroin, fentanyl, oxycodone (OxyContin), and hydrocodone (Vicodin). Some opioids are used legally, as prescription painkillers. Otherwise, people use them to manage their pain and stress, and to feel good.

Drug overdose is the main cause of death in American adults under the age of 50. In 2015, there were 52,404 overdose deaths in the United States—the worst year ever, until 2016, when around 64,000 people died. And most of these were opioid overdoses. Yet many people would use marijuana instead of narcotics, if given the chance. Marijuana, like the opioids, can reduce pain and stress and produce a sense of well-being. The legalization of *medical* marijuana has already reduced opioid fatalities, according to several studies. But legalizing marijuana generally should also save lives, for the same reason: The more widely available pot is, the more often it will be used instead of an opioid.

The benefits of legalizing marijuana clearly outweigh the harms. Therefore, almost all utilitarians favor legalization.

How Did This Happen? If alcohol is more harmful than marijuana, then cigarettes are much worse than either. Cigarettes cause almost one-fifth of deaths in the United States. Smoking kills more people than the following causes *combined*: alcohol, illegal drugs, car accidents, guns, and HIV/AIDS. Yet cigarettes are legal throughout the United States, and marijuana is not.

The utilitarian case for legalization seems so strong that one might wonder how marijuana became the main target of America's Drug War. Did the architects of that war really believe that marijuana is extremely harmful?

Evidently, they did not. In the mid-1990s, President Nixon's advisor John Ehrlichman appeared to speak frankly about why Nixon had started the War on Drugs. "You want to know what this was really all about?" he said.

> [The Nixon White House] had two enemies: the antiwar left and black people. . . . We knew we couldn't make it illegal to be either against the [Vietnam] war or black, but by getting the public to associate the hippies with marijuana and blacks with heroin, and then criminalizing both heavily, we could disrupt those communities. We could arrest their leaders, raid their homes, break up their meetings, and vilify them night after night on the evening news. Did we know we were lying about the drugs? Of course we did.

In 1974, Richard Nixon resigned the presidency in disgrace. Yet his Drug War goes on. It goes on, even though it now seems like a war that began dishonestly, with racist, partisan political motivations, and has done more harm than good.

7.4. Third Example: Nonhuman Animals

The treatment of animals has traditionally been regarded as a trivial matter. Christians believe that man alone is made in God's image and that animals do not have souls. Thus, by the natural order of things, we can treat animals in any way we like. Saint Thomas Aquinas (1225–1274) summed up the traditional view when he wrote,

> Hereby is refuted the error of those who said it is sinful for a man to kill brute animals; for by the divine providence they are intended for man's use in the natural order. Hence it is not wrong for man to make use of them, either by killing them or in any other way whatever.

But isn't it wrong to be *cruel* to animals? Aquinas concedes that it is, but he says the reason has to do with human welfare, not the welfare of the animals:

> And if any passages of Holy Scripture seem to forbid us to be cruel to brute animals, for instance to kill a bird with its young, this is either to remove man's thoughts from being cruel to other men, lest through being cruel to animals one becomes cruel to human beings; or because injury to an animal leads to the temporal hurt of man, either of the doer of the deed, or of another.

Thus, according to the traditional view, people and animals are in separate moral categories. Animals have no moral standing of their own; we are free to treat them in any way we please.

Put so bluntly, the traditional doctrine might make us a little nervous: It seems extreme in its lack of concern for nonhuman animals, many of which are, after all, intelligent and sensitive creatures. Yet much of our conduct is guided by this doctrine. We eat animals; we use them as experimental subjects in our laboratories; we use their skins for clothing and their heads as wall ornaments; we make them the objects of our amusement in circuses, rodeos, and bullfights; and we track them down and kill them for sport. All of these activities involve considerable animal pain.

If the theological "justification" of these practices seems thin, Western philosophers have offered plenty of secular ones. Philosophers have said that animals are not *rational*, that they lack the ability to *speak*, or that they are simply not *human*—and all these are given as reasons why their interests lie outside the sphere of moral concern.

The utilitarians, however, would have none of this. On their view, what matters is not whether an animal has a soul, is rational, or any of the rest. All that matters is whether it can experience happiness and unhappiness. If an animal can suffer, then we have a duty to take that into account when deciding what to do. In fact, Bentham argues that whether an animal is human or nonhuman is just as irrelevant as whether it is black or white. He writes,

> The day *may* come when the rest of the animal creation may acquire those rights which never could have been withholden

from them but by the hand of tyranny. The French have already discovered that the blackness of the skin is no reason why a human being should be abandoned without redress to the caprice of a tormentor. It may one day come to be recognized that the number of the legs, the villosity of the skin, or the termination of the *os sacrum* are reasons equally insufficient for abandoning a sensitive being to the same fate. What else is it that should trace the insuperable line? Is it the faculty of reason, or perhaps the faculty of discourse? But a full-grown horse or dog is beyond comparison a more rational, as well as a more conversable animal, than an infant of a day or a week or even a month old. But suppose they were otherwise, what would it avail? The question is not, Can they *reason*? nor Can they *talk*? but, Can they *suffer*?

If a human is tormented, why is it wrong? Because that person suffers. Similarly, if a nonhuman is tormented, it also suffers. Whether it is a *human* or an *animal* that suffers is simply irrelevant. To Bentham and Mill, this line of reasoning was conclusive. Humans and nonhumans are equally entitled to moral concern.

This view may seem as extreme, in the opposite direction, as the traditional view that grants animals no moral standing at all. Are animals really the equal of humans? In some sense, Bentham and Mill thought so, but they did not believe that animals and humans must always be treated in the same way. There are factual differences between them that will justify many differences in treatment. For example, because of their intellectual capacities, humans can take pleasure in many things that nonhumans cannot enjoy—mathematics, movies, literature, strategy games, and so on. And similarly, humans' superior capacities make them capable of frustrations and disappointments that other animals cannot experience. Thus, our duty to promote happiness entails a duty to promote those special enjoyments for humans, as well as to prevent any special harms they might suffer.

At the same time, however, we have a moral duty to take into account the suffering of animals, and their suffering should count equally with any similar suffering experienced by humans. The contrary view—that animal suffering matters less, because they're just animals—is called *speciesism*. Utilitarians believe that speciesism is discrimination against other species, just as racism is discrimination against other races.

Human beings are especially "speciesist" in their production of meat. Many people believe, in a vague way, that slaughterhouses are unpleasant, but that animals raised for food are otherwise treated humanely. In fact, farm animals live in abhorrent conditions before being taken off to slaughter. Veal calves, for example, spend 24 hours per day in pens so small that they cannot turn around, lie down comfortably, or even twist their heads around to get rid of parasites on their own bodies. The producers put them in tiny pens to save money and to keep the meat tender. The cows clearly miss their mothers, and like human infants, they want something to suck, so they try in vain to suck the sides of their wooden stalls. The calves are also fed a diet deficient in iron and roughage, in order to keep their meat pale and tasty. Their craving for iron becomes so strong that, if they're allowed to turn around, they will lick at their own urine—which normally they would never do. Without roughage, the calves cannot form a cud to chew. For this reason, they cannot be given straw bedding, because they would eat it, in an attempt to consume roughage. So, for these animals, the slaughterhouse is not an unpleasant end to an otherwise contented existence.

The veal calf is just one example. Chickens, turkeys, pigs, and adult cows all live in horrible conditions before being slaughtered. The utilitarian argument on these matters is simple. The system of meat production causes enormous suffering for the animals with no compensating benefits. Therefore, we should abandon that system. We should either become vegetarians or else treat our animals humanely before killing them.

What is most revolutionary in all this is simply the idea that nonhuman animals count. We normally assume that human beings are alone in deserving moral consideration. Utilitarianism challenges that assumption and insists that we should care about any creature that feels pleasure and pain. Human beings are special in many ways, and an adequate morality must acknowledge that fact. But we are not the only animals capable of suffering, and an adequate morality must acknowledge that fact as well.

Notes on Sources

"Priestley was the first (unless it was Beccaria) who taught my lips to pronounce this sacred truth:—That the greatest happiness of the greatest number is the foundation of morals and legislation" (Jeremy Bentham, "Extracts from Bentham's Commonplace Book," *Collected Works*, vol. 10, p. 142).

Peter Singer says that morality is not a system of nasty puritanical prohibitions in *Practical Ethics*, 2nd ed. (Cambridge: Cambridge University Press, 1993), p. 1.

Freud's death is recounted in Ronald W. Clark, *Freud: The Man and the Cause* (New York: Random House, 1980), pp. 525–527, and Paul Ferris, *Dr. Freud: A Life* (Washington, DC: Counterpoint, 1997), pp. 395–397.

Bentham is quoted from *An Introduction to the Principles of Morals and Legislation*, 1st ed. (printed in 1780; published in 1789), p. 125 (on God) and p. 311 (on animals). Bentham discusses sexual ethics in "Offences Against One's Self," written around 1785 and published posthumously.

John Stuart Mill, *On Liberty* (1859), chapter 1 ("Introductory"), paragraph 9.

Richard Nixon's "War on Drugs" speech can be read at presidency. ucsb.edu.

For statistics on incarceration and drug offenses, see the Prison Policy Initiative, "Mass Incarceration: The Whole Pie 2017" (at prison-policy.org), and E. Ann Carson and Elizabeth Anderson, "Prisoners in 2015," released in December 2016 by the U.S. Bureau of Justice Statistics, at bjs.gov.

On drugs arrests in 2010, see the American Civil Liberties Union (ACLU), "The War on Marijuana in Black and White: Billions of Dollars Wasted on Racially Biased Arrests," released in June 2013.

52% have tried pot, 22% currently use it: "Weed and the American Family," a Yahoo News/Marist Poll released in April 2017.

The marijuana nicknames are from drugabuse.gov (accessed August 13, 2017).

Over 20% of Americans live in states where pot is legal: tabulated from U.S. Census Bureau data (regarding July 1, 2016) at a time when marijuana was legal in Alaska, California, Colorado, Maine, Massachusetts, Nevada, Oregon, and Washington.

Broad support for marijuana reform: see the CBS poll released on April 20, 2017.

On marijuana and violence: 23% of Americans believe that legalizing pot increases violent crime (CBS poll, April 20, 2017).

On marijuana and addiction, see Robert Gore and Mitch Earleywine, "Marijuana's Perceived Addictiveness: A Survey of Clinicians and Researchers," in *Pot Politics: Marijuana and the Costs of Prohibition*, edited by Mitch Earleywine (Oxford University Press, 2007), pp. 176–186 (pot is less addictive than caffeine and alcohol: p. 179).

On the health effects of marijuana, see the National Academies report, "The Health Effects of Cannabis and Cannabinoids" (January 2017). On the gums, see W. Murray Thomson et al., "Cannabis Smoking and Periodontal Disease among Young Adults," *Journal of the American Medical Association*, vol. 299, no. 5 (February 6, 2008), pp. 525-531.

On marijuana and driving, see the National Academies report (cited above), and the U.S. Department of Transportation's National Highway Traffic Safety Administration report by Richard P. Compton and Amy Beming, "Drug and Alcohol Crash Risk" (February 2015).

In 2015, there were 574,641 arrests for marijuana possession, and 505,681 for violent crimes: Timothy Williams, "Marijuana Arrests Outnumber Those for Violent Crimes," *The New York Times*, October 12, 2016. On charging fees to arrestees, see Adam Liptak, "Charged a Fee for Getting Arrested, Whether Guilty or Not," *The New York Times*, December 26, 2016.

On Colorado and cannabis, see Miles Light, Adam Orens, Jacob Rowberry, and Clinton W. Salaga, "The Economic Impact of Marijuana Legalization in Colorado," released by Marijuana Policy Group in October 2016.

Black adults are over four times more likely to be arrested: see the American Civil Liberties Union (ACLU), "The War on Marijuana in Black and White: Billions of Dollars Wasted on Racially Biased Arrests," released in June 2013.

The statistics about alcohol are from CDC.gov, "Fact Sheets—Alcohol Use and Your Health" (accessed July 23, 2017).

On the opioid crisis, see Josh Katz, "Drug Deaths in America Are Rising Faster Than Ever," *The New York Times* (June 5, 2017); Margaret Talbot, "The Addicts Next Door," *The New Yorker*, June 5 and 12, 2017; and Lenny Bernstein, "Deaths from drug overdoses soared in the first nine months of 2016," *The Washington Post* (August 8, 2017).

On opioids and marijuana, see Yuyan Shi, "Medical Marijuana Policies and Hospitalizations Related to Marijuana and Opioid Pain Reliever," *Drug and Alcohol Dependence*, vol. 173 (April 1, 2017), pp. 144-150, and Marcus A. Bachhuber et al., "Medical Cannabis Laws and Opioid Analgesic Overdose Mortality in the United States, 1999-2010," *JAMA Internal Medicine*, October 2014 (vol. 174, no. 10), pp. 1668-1673.

The facts about smoking are from cdc.gov ("Health Effects of Cigarette Smoking").

John Ehrlichman was quoted by Dan Baum in "How to Win the War on Drugs: Legalize It All," *Harper's*, April 2016.

Aquinas on animals: see *Summa Contra Gentiles*, book 3, chapter 112. In the *Basic Writings of St. Thomas Aquinas*, edited by Anton C. Pegis (New York: Random House, 1945), vol. 2, see p. 222.

CHAPTER 8

The Debate over Utilitarianism

The creed which accepts . . . the Greatest Happiness Principle . . . holds that actions are right . . . as they tend to promote happiness, wrong as they tend to produce the reverse of happiness.

JOHN STUART MILL, *UTILITARIANISM* (1861)

Man does not strive after happiness; only the Englishman does that.

FRIEDRICH NIETZSCHE, *TWILIGHT OF THE IDOLS* (1889)

8.1. The Classical Version of the Theory

Classical Utilitarianism can be summed up in three propositions: (a) The morality of an action depends solely on the consequences of the action; nothing else matters. (b) An action's consequences matter only insofar as they involve the greater or lesser happiness of individuals. (c) In the assessment of consequences, each individual's happiness gets *equal consideration*. This means that equal amounts of happiness always count equally; nobody's well-being matters more just because he is rich, let's say, or powerful, or handsome, or a man rather than a woman. Morally, everyone counts the same. According to Classical Utilitarianism, an action is right if it produces the greatest overall balance of happiness over unhappiness.

Classical Utilitarianism was developed and defended by three of the greatest philosophers in 19th-century England: Jeremy Bentham (1748–1832), John Stuart Mill (1806–1873), and Henry Sidgwick (1838–1900). Thanks in part to their work, Utilitarianism has had a profound influence on modern thinking. Most moral philosophers, however, reject the theory. In what follows, we will discuss some of the objections that have made the theory unpopular. In examining these arguments, we will also be pondering some of the deepest questions in ethical theory.

8.2. Is Pleasure All That Matters?

The question, *What things are good?* is different from the question, *What actions are right?* and Utilitarianism answers the second question by reference to the first. Right actions are the ones that produce the most good. But what is good? The utilitarian reply is: happiness. As Mill puts it, "The utilitarian doctrine is that happiness is desirable, and the only thing desirable, as an end; all other things being only desirable as means to that end."

But what is happiness? According to the classical utilitarians, happiness is pleasure. Utilitarians understand "pleasure" broadly, to include all mental states that feel good. A sense of accomplishment, a delicious taste, and the heightened awareness that comes at the climax of a suspenseful movie are all examples of pleasure. The thesis that pleasure is the one ultimate good—and pain the one ultimate evil—has been known since antiquity as Hedonism. The idea that things are good or bad because of how they make us *feel* has always had a following in philosophy. Yet a little reflection seems to reveal flaws in this idea.

Consider these two examples:

- *You think someone is your friend, but he ridicules you behind your back.* No one tells you, so you never know. Is this unfortunate for you? Hedonists would have to say it is not, because you are never caused any pain. Yet we believe that something bad is going on. You are being mistreated, even though you are unaware of it and suffer no unhappiness.
- *A promising young pianist's hands are injured in a car accident so that she can no longer play.* Why is this bad for her? Hedonists would say it is bad because it causes her pain and eliminates a source of joy for her. But suppose she finds something else that she enjoys just as much—suppose, for example, she gets as much pleasure from watching hockey on TV as she once got from playing the piano. Why

is her accident now a tragedy? Or why is it a bad thing at all? The hedonist can only say that she will feel frustrated and upset whenever she thinks of what might have been, and *that* is her misfortune. But this explanation gets things backward. It is not as though, by feeling upset, she has turned a neutral situation into a bad one. On the contrary, the bad situation is what made her unhappy. She might have become a great pianist, and now she will not. We cannot eliminate the tragedy by getting her to cheer up and watch hockey.

Both of these examples rely on the same idea: We value things other than pleasure. For example, we value artistic creativity and friendship. These things make us happy, but that's not the only reason we value them. It seems like a misfortune to lose them, even if there is no loss of happiness.

For this reason, most present-day utilitarians reject the classical assumption of Hedonism. Some of them bypass the question of what's good, saying only that right actions are the ones that have the best results, however that is measured. Other utilitarians, such as the English philosopher G. E. Moore (1873–1958), have compiled short lists of things to be regarded as valuable in themselves. Moore suggested that there are three intrinsic goods—pleasure, friendship, and aesthetic enjoyment—and so right actions are actions that maximize the world's supply of those things. Still others say that we should help people get what they *want*—in other words, we should try to maximize the satisfaction of people's *preferences*. We won't discuss these theories any further. I mention them only to note that, although Hedonism has largely been rejected, contemporary utilitarians have not found it hard to carry on.

8.3. Are Consequences All That Matter?

To determine whether an action is right, utilitarians believe that we should look at *what will happen as a result of doing it*. This idea is central to the theory. If things other than consequences are important in determining what is right, then Utilitarianism is incorrect. Here are three arguments that attack the theory at just this point.

Justice. In 1965, writing in the racially charged climate of the American civil rights movement, H. J. McCloskey asks us to consider the following case:

> Suppose a utilitarian were visiting an area in which there was racial strife, and that, during his visit, a Negro rapes a white woman, and that race riots occur as a result of the crime. . . . Suppose too that our utilitarian is in the area of the crime when it is committed such that his testimony would bring about the conviction of [whomever he accuses]. If he knows that a quick arrest will stop the riots and lynchings, surely, as a utilitarian, he must conclude that he has a duty to bear false witness in order to bring about the punishment of an innocent person.

Such an accusation would have bad consequences—the innocent man would be convicted—but there would be enough good consequences to outweigh them: The riots and lynchings would be stopped, and many lives would be saved. The best outcome would thus be achieved by bearing false witness; therefore, according to Utilitarianism, lying is the thing to do. But, the argument continues, it would be wrong to bring about the conviction of an innocent person. Therefore, Utilitarianism must be incorrect.

According to the critics of Utilitarianism, this argument illustrates one of the theory's most serious shortcomings, namely, that it conflicts with the ideal of justice. Justice requires us to treat people fairly, according to the merits of their particular situations. In McCloskey's example, Utilitarianism requires that we treat someone unfairly. Therefore, Utilitarianism cannot be right.

Rights. Here is an example from the U.S. Court of Appeals. In the case of *York v. Story* (1963), arising out of California,

> In October, 1958, appellant [Ms. Angelynn York] went to the police department of Chino for the purpose of filing charges in connection with an assault upon her. Appellee Ron Story, an officer of that police department, then acting under color of his authority as such, advised appellant that it was necessary to take photographs of her. Story then took appellant to a room in the police station, locked the door, and directed her to undress, which she did. Story then directed appellant to assume various indecent positions, and photographed her in those

positions. These photographs were not made for any lawful or legitimate purpose.

Appellant objected to undressing. She stated to Story that there was no need to take photographs of her in the nude, or in the positions she was directed to take, because the bruises would not show in any photograph. . . .

Later that month, Story advised appellant that the pictures did not come out and that he had destroyed them. Instead, Story [made additional prints and] circulated these photographs among the personnel of the Chino police department.

Ms. York brought suit against Officer Story and won. Her legal rights had clearly been violated. But what about the *morality* of Story's behavior? Utilitarianism says that actions are defensible if they produce a favorable balance of happiness over unhappiness. This suggests that we compare the amount of unhappiness caused to York with the amount of pleasure the photographs gave to Officer Story and the others. And it is at least possible that more happiness than unhappiness was created. In that case, the utilitarian would say that Story's actions were morally acceptable. But this seems perverse. Why should the pleasure of Story and his friends matter at all? They had no right to treat York in this way, and the fact that they enjoyed doing so hardly seems relevant.

Consider a related case. Suppose a Peeping Tom spied on a woman through her bedroom window and secretly took pictures of her undressed. Suppose he is never caught, and he never shows the pictures to anyone. Under these circumstances, the only consequence of his action seems to be an increase in his own happiness. No one else, including the woman, is caused any unhappiness at all. How, then, could a utilitarian deny that the Peeping Tom's actions are right? Utilitarianism again appears to be unacceptable.

The key point is that Utilitarianism is at odds with the idea that people have *rights* that may not be trampled on merely because one anticipates good results. In these examples, the woman's right to privacy is violated. But we could think of similar cases in which other rights are at issue—the right to worship freely, the right to speak one's mind, or even the right to live. On Utilitarianism, an individual's rights may always be trampled upon if enough people benefit from the trampling. Utilitarianism has thus been accused of supporting the "tyranny of the majority": If the majority of people would take pleasure in someone's rights being abused, then those rights should be abused, because the pleasure of the majority outweighs the suffering of the one. However, we do not think that our individual rights should mean so little, morally. The notion of an individual right is not a utilitarian notion. Quite the opposite: It is a notion that places limits on how an individual may be treated, regardless of the good that might be accomplished.

Backward-Looking Reasons. Suppose you have promised to do something—say, you promised to meet your friend at a coffee shop this afternoon. But when the time comes to go, you don't want to; you need to catch up on some work and would rather stay home. You start to cancel the get-together by text, but then you remember that your friend just lost her smartphone. What should you do?

Suppose you judge that the benefits of staying home would outweigh, however slightly, the irritation that your friend would feel from being stood up. If you applied the utilitarian standard to this situation, then you might conclude that you should stay home and stand up your friend. Yet that conclusion seems incorrect. *The fact that you promised to be at the coffee shop* imposes an obligation on you that you cannot shed so easily.

Of course, if a great deal were at stake—if, for example, you had to rush your roommate to the hospital—then you should break your promise. However, a small gain in happiness cannot overcome your obligation to keep your word. After all, a promise should mean *something*, morally. Thus, once again, Utilitarianism seems mistaken.

This criticism is possible because Utilitarianism cares only about the *consequences* of our actions. However, we normally think that some facts about the past are important, too. You made a promise to your friend, and that's about the past. Utilitarianism seems faulty because it excludes such backward-looking reasons.

Once we understand this point, we can think of other examples of backward-looking reasons. The fact that someone committed a crime is a reason to punish him. The fact that someone did you a favor last week is a reason for you to do her a favor next week. The fact that you hurt someone yesterday is a reason to apologize to him today. These are all facts about the past that are relevant to determining our obligations. But Utilitarianism makes the past irrelevant, and so it seems flawed.

8.4. Should We Be Equally Concerned for Everyone?

The last part of Utilitarianism says that we must treat each person's happiness as equally important—or as Mill put it, we must be "as strictly impartial as a disinterested and benevolent spectator." Stated abstractly, this sounds plausible, but it has troubling implications. One problem is that the requirement of "equal concern" places too great a demand on us; another problem is that it tells us to do things that would destroy our personal relationships.

The Charge That Utilitarianism Is Too Demanding. Suppose you are on your way to the movies when someone points out that the money you are about to spend could be used to feed the starving or to provide inoculations for third-world children. Surely, those people need food and medicine more than you need to see Vin Diesel and Dwayne "The Rock" Johnson. So you forgo your entertainment and donate your money to charity. But it doesn't stop there. By the same reasoning, you cannot buy nice shoes or upgrade to a new computer. And you should probably eat out less and move into a cheaper apartment. After all, what's more important—your luxuries or children's lives?

In fact, faithful adherence to the utilitarian standard would require you to give away your wealth until you've made yourself as poor as the people you're helping. Or rather, you'd need to leave yourself just enough to maintain your job, so that you can keep on giving. Although we would admire someone who did all this, we would not think that such a person was merely "doing his duty." Rather, we would regard him as a saint, as someone whose generosity went *beyond* the call of duty. Philosophers call such actions *supererogatory*. But Utilitarianism seems unable to recognize this moral category.

The problem is not merely that Utilitarianism would require us to give away most of our things. It would also prevent us from carrying on with our lives. We all have goals and projects that make our lives meaningful. But an ethic that requires us to promote the general welfare to the maximum extent possible would force us to abandon those endeavors. Suppose you are a Web designer, not getting rich but making a decent living; you have two children whom you love; and on weekends, you like to perform with an amateur theater group. In addition, you enjoy reading history. How could there be anything wrong with this? But judged by the utilitarian standard, you are leading an immoral life. After all, you could do a lot more good by spending your time in other ways.

The Charge That Utilitarianism Disrupts Our Personal Relationships. In practice, none of us is willing to treat everyone equally, because that would require us to give up our special ties to friends and family. We are all deeply partial where our family and friends are concerned. We love them, and we go to great lengths to help them. To us, they are not just members of the great crowd of humanity—they are special. But all this is inconsistent with impartiality. When you are impartial, you miss out on intimacy, love, affection, and friendship.

At this point, Utilitarianism seems to have lost all touch with reality. What would it be like to care about one's spouse no more than one cares about complete strangers? The very idea is absurd; not only is it profoundly contrary to normal human emotions, but loving relationships could not even exist apart from special responsibilities and obligations. Again, what would it be like to treat one's children with no greater love than one has for strangers? As John Cottingham puts it, "A parent who leaves his child to burn" because "the building contains someone else whose future contribution to the general welfare promises to be greater, is not a hero; he is (rightly) an object of moral contempt, a moral leper."

8.5. The Defense of Utilitarianism

Together, these objections appear to be decisive. Utilitarianism seems unconcerned with both justice and individual rights. Moreover, it cannot account for backward-looking reasons. If we lived by the theory, we would become poor, and we would have to stop loving our family and our friends.

Most philosophers have, therefore, abandoned Utilitarianism. Some philosophers, however, still believe it. They defend it in three different ways.

The First Defense: Contesting the Consequences. Most of the arguments against Utilitarianism go like this: A situation is described; then it is said that some particular (vile!) action would have the best consequences under those circumstances; then Utilitarianism is faulted for advocating that action. These arguments, however, succeed only if the actions they describe really would have the best consequences. Would they? According to the first defense, they would not.

Consider, for example, McCloskey's argument, in which Utilitarianism is supposed to support framing an innocent man in order to stop a race riot. In the real world, would bearing false witness in this way actually have good consequences? Probably not. The liar might be discovered, and then the situation would be worse than before. And even if the lie succeeded, the real culprit would remain at large and might commit more crimes, to be followed by more riots. Moreover, if the guilty party were later caught, which is always possible, the liar would be in deep trouble, and public trust in the criminal justice system would erode. The moral is that although one might *think* that one can bring about the best consequences by such behavior, experience teaches the opposite: Utility is not served by framing innocent people.

The same goes for the other arguments. Lying, violating people's rights, breaking one's promises, and severing one's intimate relationships all have bad consequences. Only in philosophers' imaginations is it otherwise. In the real world, Peeping Toms are caught, just as Officer Story was caught, and their victims pay the price. In the real world, when people lie, their reputations suffer and other people get hurt; and when people break their promises and fail to return favors, they lose their friends.

So that is the first defense. Unfortunately, it is not very effective. While it is true that *most* acts of false witness and the like have bad consequences, it cannot be said that *all* such acts have bad consequences. At least once in a while, one can bring about a good result by doing something repugnant to moral common sense.

Therefore, in at least some real-life cases, Utilitarianism will conflict with common sense. Moreover, even if the anti-utilitarian arguments had to rely on fictitious examples, those arguments would retain their power. Theories like Utilitarianism are supposed to apply to *all* situations, including situations that are merely hypothetical. Thus, showing that Utilitarianism has unacceptable implications in made-up cases is a valid way of critiquing it. The first defense, then, is weak.

The Second Defense: The Principle of Utility Is a Guide for Choosing Rules, Not Acts. Revising a theory is a two-step process: first, you identify which feature of the theory needs work; second, you change only that feature, leaving the rest of the theory intact. What feature of Classical Utilitarianism is causing the trouble?

The troublesome assumption might be that *each individual action* should be judged by the utilitarian standard. Whether it would be wrong to tell a particular lie depends on the consequences of *telling that particular lie;* whether you should keep a particular promise depends on the consequences of *keeping that particular promise;* and so on for each of the examples we have considered. If what we care about is the consequences of particular actions, then we can always dream up circumstances in which a horrific action will have the best consequences.

Therefore, the new version of Utilitarianism modifies the theory so that individual actions are no longer judged by the Principle of Utility. Instead, we must first ask what *set of rules* is optimal, from a utilitarian viewpoint. In other words, what rules should we follow in order to maximize happiness? Individual acts are then assessed according to whether they abide by these rules. This new version of the theory is called "Rule-Utilitarianism," to distinguish it from the original theory, now commonly called "Act-Utilitarianism."

Rule-Utilitarianism has an easy answer to the anti-utilitarian arguments. An act-utilitarian would incriminate the innocent man in McCloskey's example because the consequences of *that particular act* would be good. But the rule-utilitarian would not reason in that way. She would first ask, "What rules of conduct tend to promote the most happiness?" And one good rule is "don't bear false witness against the innocent." That rule is simple and easy to remember, and following it will almost always increase happiness. By appealing to it, the rule-utilitarian can conclude that in McCloskey's example we should not testify against the innocent man.

Similar reasoning can be used to establish rules against violating people's rights, breaking promises, lying, betraying one's friends, and so on. We should accept such rules because following them, on a regular basis, promotes the general happiness. So we no longer judge acts by their utility but by their conformity to these rules. Thus, Rule-Utilitarianism cannot be convicted of violating our moral common sense. In shifting the emphasis from the justification of acts to the justification of rules, Utilitarianism has been brought into line with our intuitive judgments.

However, a serious problem with Rule-Utilitarianism arises when we ask whether the ideal rules have *exceptions*. Must the rules be followed no matter what? What if a "forbidden" act would greatly increase the overall good? The rule-utilitarian might give any one of three answers to this question.

First, if she says that in such cases we may violate the rules, then it looks like she wants to assess actions on a case-by-case basis. This is Act-Utilitarianism, not Rule-Utilitarianism. Thus, it is vulnerable to all of the objections that have been given.

Second, she might suggest that we formulate the rules so that violating them will never increase happiness. For example, instead of using the rule, "don't bear false witness against the innocent," we might use the rule, "don't bear false witness against the innocent, unless doing so would achieve some great good." If we change all of the rules in this way, then Rule-Utilitarianism will be exactly like Act-Utilitarianism in practice; the rules we follow will always tell us to choose the act that generates the most happiness. But now Rule-Utilitarianism does not provide a response to the anti-utilitarian arguments; like Act-Utilitarianism, Rule-Utilitarianism tells us to incriminate the innocent, break our promises, spy on people in their homes, and so on.

Finally, the rule-utilitarian might stand her ground and say that we should never break the rules, even to promote happiness. J. J. C. Smart (1920–2012) says that such a person suffers from an irrational "rule worship." Whatever one thinks of that, this version of Rule-Utilitarianism is not really a utilitarian theory at all.

Utilitarians care solely about happiness and about consequences, but this theory, in addition, cares about following rules. The theory is thus a mixture of Utilitarianism and something else entirely. To paraphrase one writer, this type of Rule-Utilitarianism is like a rubber duck: Just as a rubber duck is not a kind of duck, this type of Rule-Utilitarianism is not a kind of Utilitarianism. And so, we cannot defend Utilitarianism by appealing to it.

The Third Defense: "Common Sense" Is Wrong. Finally, some utilitarians have offered a very different response to the objections. Upon being told that Utilitarianism conflicts with common sense, they respond, "So what?" Looking back at his own defense of Utilitarianism, J. J. C. Smart writes,

> Admittedly utilitarianism does have consequences which are incompatible with the common moral consciousness, but I tended to take the view "so much the worse for the common moral consciousness." That is, I was inclined to reject the common methodology of testing general ethical principles by seeing how they square with our feelings in particular instances.

This breed of utilitarian—hard-nosed and unapologetic—can offer three responses to the anti-utilitarian arguments.

The First Response: All Values Have a Utilitarian Basis. Critics of Utilitarianism say that the theory can't make sense of some of our most important values—such as the value we attach to truth telling, promise keeping, respecting other people's privacy, and loving our children. Consider, for example, lying. The main reason not to lie, the critics say, has nothing to do with bad consequences. The reason is that lying is dishonest; it betrays people's trust. That fact has nothing to do with the utilitarian calculation of benefits and harms. Honesty has a value over and above any value that the utilitarian can acknowledge. And the same is true of promise keeping, respecting other people's privacy, and loving our children.

But according to philosophers such as Smart, we should think about these values one at a time and consider why they're important. When people lie, the lies are often discovered, and those betrayed feel hurt and angry. When people break their promises, they irritate their neighbors and alienate their friends. Someone whose privacy is violated may feel humiliated and want to withdraw from others. When people don't care more about their own children than they do about strangers, their children feel unloved, and one day they too may become unloving parents. All these things reduce happiness. Far from being at odds with the idea that we should be honest, dependable, respectful, and loving to our children, Utilitarianism explains why those things are good.

Moreover, apart from the utilitarian explanation, these duties would seem inexplicable. What could be stranger than saying that lying is wrong "in itself," apart from the harm that lying causes? And how could people have a "right to privacy" unless respecting that right brought about some benefit? On this way of thinking, Utilitarianism is not incompatible with common sense; on the contrary, Utilitarianism justifies the commonsense values we have.

The Second Response: Our Gut Reactions Can't Be Trusted When Cases Are Exceptional. Although some cases of injustice serve the common good, those cases are exceptions. Lying, promise breaking, and violations of privacy usually lead to unhappiness, not happiness. This observation forms the basis of another utilitarian response.

Consider again McCloskey's example of the person who is tempted to bear false witness. Why do we immediately and instinctively believe it to be wrong to bear false witness against an innocent person? The reason, some say, is that throughout our lives we have seen lies lead to misery and misfortune. Thus, *we instinctively condemn all lies.* But when we condemn lies that are beneficial, our intuitive faculties are misfiring. Experience has taught us to condemn lies because they reduce happiness. Now, however, we are condemning lies that increase happiness. When confronting unusual cases, such as McCloskey's, perhaps we should trust the Principle of Utility more than our gut instincts.

The Third Response: We Should Focus on *All* the Consequences. When we're asked to consider a "despicable" action that maximizes happiness, the action is often presented in a way that encourages us to focus on its bad effects, rather than on its good effects. If instead we focus on *all* the effects of the act, Utilitarianism will seem more plausible.

THE DEBATE OVER UTILITARIANISM   131

Consider yet again the McCloskey example. McCloskey says that it would be wrong to convict an innocent man because that would be unjust. But what about the *other* innocent people who will be hurt if the rioting and lynchings continue? What about the pain that will be endured by those who are beaten and tormented by the mob? What about the deaths that will occur if the man doesn't lie? Children will lose their parents, and parents will lose their children. Of course, we never want to face a situation like this. But if we must choose between securing the conviction of one innocent person and allowing the deaths of several innocent people, is it so unreasonable to think that the first option is preferable?

And consider again the objection that Utilitarianism is too demanding because it tells us to use our resources to feed starving children instead of using those resources on ourselves. If we focus our thoughts on those who would starve, do the demands of Utilitarianism seem so unreasonable? Isn't it self-serving of us to say that Utilitarianism is "too demanding," rather than saying that we should do more to help?

This strategy works better for some cases than for others. Consider the Peeping Tom. The unapologetic utilitarian will tell us to consider the pleasure *he* gets from spying on unsuspecting women. If he gets away with it, what harm has been done? Why should his action be condemned? Most people will condemn his behavior, despite the utilitarian arguments. Utilitarianism, as Smart suggests, cannot be fully reconciled with common sense. Whether the theory needs such a reconciliation remains an open question.

8.6. Concluding Thoughts

If we consult what Smart calls our "common moral consciousness," many considerations other than utility seem morally important. But Smart is right to warn us that "common sense" cannot be trusted. That may turn out to be Utilitarianism's greatest insight. The deficiencies of moral common sense become obvious if we think about it. Many white people once felt that there was an important difference between whites and blacks, so that the interests of whites were somehow more important. Trusting the "common sense" of their day, they might have insisted that an adequate moral theory should accommodate this "fact." Today, no one worth listening to says such things, but who knows how many other irrational prejudices are still part of our moral common sense? At the end of his classic study of race relations, *An American Dilemma*, Nobel laureate Gunnar Myrdal (1898–1987) reminds us:

> There must be still other countless errors of the same sort that no living man can yet detect, because of the fog within which our type of Western culture envelops us. Cultural influences have set up the assumptions about the mind, the body, and the universe with which we begin; pose the questions we ask; influence the facts we seek; determine the interpretation we give these facts; and direct our reaction to these interpretations and conclusions.

Could it be, for example, that future generations will look back in disgust at the way affluent people in the 21st century enjoyed their comfortable lives while third-world children died of easily preventable diseases? If so, they might note that utilitarian philosophers were ahead of their time in condemning it.

Notes on Sources

"The utilitarian doctrine is that happiness is desirable . . .": John Stuart Mill, *Utilitarianism* (1861; available in various reprintings), chapter 4, para. 2.

G. E. Moore discusses what has intrinsic value in the last chapter of *Principia Ethica* (Cambridge: Cambridge University Press, 1903).

McCloskey's example of the utilitarian tempted to bear false witness: "A Non-Utilitarian Approach to Punishment," *Inquiry* 8 (1965), pp. 239–255.

"As strictly impartial as a disinterested and benevolent spectator": John Stuart Mill, *Utilitarianism* (1861), chapter 2, para. 18.

John Cottingham, "Partialism, Favouritism and Morality," *Philosophical Quarterly* 36 (1986), p. 357.

Smart is quoted from J. J. C. Smart and Bernard Williams, *Utilitarianism: For and Against* (Cambridge: Cambridge University Press, 1973), p. 68. He discusses "rule worship" on p. 10.

Frances Howard-Snyder, "Rule Consequentialism Is a Rubber Duck," *American Philosophical Quarterly* 30 (1993), pp. 271–278.

Gunnar Myrdal, *An American Dilemma: The Negro Problem and American Democracy* (1944; available in various reprintings).

CHAPTER 9

*A*re There Absolute Moral Rules?

You may not do evil that good may come.
SAINT PAUL, *LETTER TO THE ROMANS* (ca. A.D. 50)

9.1. Harry Truman and Elizabeth Anscombe

Harry S. Truman will always be remembered as the man who made the decision to drop the atomic bombs on Hiroshima and Nagasaki. When he became president in 1945, following the death of Franklin D. Roosevelt, Truman knew nothing about the bomb; Roosevelt's advisors had to fill him in. The Allies were winning the war in the Pacific, they said, but at a terrible cost. Plans had been drawn up for an invasion of Japan, but that battle would be even bloodier than the D-Day assault on Normandy, France, had been. Using the atomic bomb on one or two Japanese cities might bring the war to a speedy end, making the invasion unnecessary.

At first Truman was reluctant to use the new weapon. The problem was that each bomb would obliterate an entire city—not just the military targets, but the hospitals, schools, and homes. Women, children, old people, and other noncombatants would be wiped out along with the military personnel. The Allies had bombed cities before, but Truman sensed that the new weapon made the issue of noncombatant deaths more acute. Moreover, the United States was on record as condemning attacks on civilian targets. In 1939, before America had entered the war, President Roosevelt had sent a message to the governments of France, Germany, Italy, Poland, and

Great Britain, denouncing the bombardment of cities in the strongest terms. He had called it an "inhuman barbarism":

> The ruthless bombing from the air of civilians . . . which has resulted in the maiming and in the death of thousands of defenseless men, women, and children, has sickened the hearts of every civilized man and woman, and has profoundly shocked the conscience of humanity. If resort is had to this form of inhuman barbarism during the period of the tragic conflagration with which the world is now confronted, hundreds of thousands of innocent human beings who have no responsibility for, and who are not even remotely participating in, the hostilities which have now broken out, will lose their lives.

Truman expressed similar thoughts when he decided to authorize the bombings. He wrote in his diary, "I have told the Sec. of War, Mr. Stimson, to use it so that military objectives and soldiers and sailors are the target and not women and children. . . . The target will be a purely military one." It is hard to know what to make of this, because Truman knew that the bombs would destroy whole cities. Nonetheless, it is clear that he was worried about the issue of noncombatants.

It is also clear that Truman was sure of his decision. Winston Churchill, the wartime leader of Great Britain, met with Truman shortly before the bombs were dropped. "The decision whether or not to use the atomic bomb," Churchill later wrote, ". . . was never even an issue. There was unanimous, automatic, unquestioned agreement around our table." Truman said that he "slept like a baby" after signing the final order.

Elizabeth Anscombe, who died in 2001, was a 20-year-old student at Oxford University when World War II began. At that time, she co-authored a pamphlet arguing that Britain should not go to war because countries at war inevitably end up fighting by unjust means. "Miss Anscombe," as she was always known—despite her 59-year marriage and her seven children—would go on to become one of the 20th century's most distinguished philosophers and perhaps the greatest woman philosopher in history.

Miss Anscombe was also a Catholic, and her religion was central to her life. Her ethical views reflected traditional Catholic teachings. In 1968, after Pope Paul VI affirmed the church's ban on contraception, she wrote a pamphlet explaining why artificial birth control is immoral. Late in her life, she was arrested while protesting outside a British abortion clinic. She also accepted the church's teaching about the ethical conduct of war, which brought her into conflict with Truman.

Truman and Anscombe crossed paths in 1956. Oxford University was planning to grant Truman an honorary degree in thanks for America's wartime help, and those proposing the honor assumed that it would be uncontroversial. But Anscombe and two other faculty members opposed the idea. Although they lost, they forced a vote on what would otherwise have been a rubber-stamp approval. Then, while the degree was being conferred, Anscombe knelt outside the hall, praying.

Anscombe wrote another pamphlet, this time explaining that Truman was a murderer because he had ordered the bombings of Hiroshima and Nagasaki. Truman, of course, thought the bombings were justified because they had shortened the war and saved lives. For Anscombe, this was not good enough. "For men to choose to kill the innocent as a means to their ends," she wrote, "is always murder." To the argument that the bombings saved more lives than they took, she replied, "Come now: if you had to choose between boiling one baby and letting some frightful disaster befall a thousand people—or a million people, if a thousand is not enough—what would you do?"

Anscombe's example was apt. The bomb blast at Hiroshima, which ignited birds in midair, did lead to babies being boiled: People died in rivers, reservoirs, and cisterns, trying in vain to escape the heat. Anscombe's point was that *some things may not be done, no matter what.* It does not matter if we could accomplish some great good by boiling a baby; it is simply wrong. Anscombe believed in a host of such rules. Under no circumstances, she said, may we intentionally kill innocent people; worship idols; make a false profession of faith; engage in sodomy or adultery; punish one person for the acts of another; or commit treachery, which she describes as "obtaining a man's confidence in a grave matter by promises of trustworthy friendship and then betraying him to his enemies." This list, of course, is Anscombe's; other people may believe in different exceptionless or "absolute" moral rules.

9.2. The Categorical Imperative

The idea that moral rules have no exceptions is hard to defend. It is easy enough to explain why we sometimes *should* break a rule—we can simply point to cases in which following the rule would have terrible consequences. But how can we defend *not* breaking the rule in such cases? We might say that moral rules are God's inviolable commands. Apart from that, what can be said?

Before the 20th century, there was one major philosopher who believed that moral rules are absolute. Immanuel Kant (1724–1804) argued that lying is wrong under any circumstances. He did not appeal to religion; instead, he held that lying is forbidden by reason itself. To see how he reached this conclusion, let's look at his general theory of ethics.

Kant observed that the word *ought* is often used nonmorally:

- If you want to become a better chess player, you *ought* to study the games of Magnus Carlsen.
- If you want to go to college, you *ought* to take the SAT.

Much of our conduct is governed by such "oughts." The pattern is this: We have a certain desire (to become a better chess player, to go to college); we recognize that a certain course of action will help us get what we want (studying Carlsen's games, taking the SAT); and so we follow the indicated plan.

Kant called these "hypothetical imperatives" because they tell us what to do *provided that* we have the relevant desires. A person who did not want to improve her chess would have no reason to study Carlsen's games; someone who did not want to go to college would have no reason to take the SAT. Because the binding force of the "ought" depends on having the relevant desire, we can escape its grip by letting go of the desire. So, for example, I can avoid taking the SAT by deciding that I don't want to go to college.

Moral obligations, by contrast, do not depend on having particular desires. The form of a moral obligation is not "*if* you want so-and-so, then you ought to do such-and-such." Instead, moral requirements are *categorical:* They have the form, "You ought to do such-and-such, *period.*" The moral rule is not, for example, that you ought to help people *if* you care about them or *if* you want to be a good person. Instead, the rule is that you should help people *no matter what* your desires are. That is why moral requirements cannot be escaped by saying "I don't care about that."

Hypothetical "oughts" are easy to understand. They merely tell us to do what is necessary to achieve our goals. Categorical "oughts," on the other hand, are mysterious. How can we be obligated to behave in a certain way regardless of our goals? Kant has an answer. Just as hypothetical "oughts" are possible because we have *desires*, categorical "oughts" are possible because we have *reason*. Categorical oughts, Kant says, are derived from a principle that every rational person must accept: the Categorical Imperative. In his *Foundations of the Metaphysics of Morals* (1785), Kant expresses the Categorical Imperative as follows:

> Act only according to that maxim by which you can at the same time will that it should become a universal law.

This principle provides a way to tell whether an act is morally allowed. When you are thinking about doing something, ask what rule you would be following if you actually did it. This rule will be the "maxim" of your act. Then ask whether you would be willing for your maxim to become a universal law. In other words, would you allow your rule to be followed by all people at all times? If so, then your maxim is sound, and your act is acceptable. But if not, then your act is forbidden.

Kant gives several examples of how this works. Suppose, he says, a man needs money, but no one will lend it to him unless he promises to pay it back—which he knows he won't be able to do. Should he make a false promise to get the loan? If he did, his maxim would be: *Whenever you need a loan, promise to repay it, even if you know you can't.* Now, could he will that this rule become a universal law? Obviously not, because it would be self-defeating. Once this rule became a universal practice, no one would believe such promises, and so no one would make loans based on them.

Kant gives another example, about giving aid. Suppose, he says, I refuse to help others in need, saying to myself, "What do I care? Let each person fend for himself." This, again, is a rule that I cannot will to be a universal law. For at some point in my life, I will need the help of others, and I will not want them to turn away from me.

9.3. Kant's Arguments on Lying

According to Kant, then, our behavior should be guided by universal laws, which are moral rules that hold true in all circumstances. Kant believed in many such exceptionless rules. We'll focus on the rule against lying, which Kant had especially strong feelings about. He said that lying under any circumstances is "the obliteration of one's dignity as a human being."

Kant offered two arguments for an absolute or exceptionless rule against lying.

1. His main argument relies on the Categorical Imperative. We could not will a universal law that allows us to lie, Kant said, because such a law would be self-defeating. As soon as lying became common, people would stop believing each other. Lying would then have no point, and in a sense lying would become impossible, because nobody would pay attention to what is said. Therefore, Kant reasoned, lying cannot be allowed. And so, it is forbidden under any circumstances.

This argument has a flaw, which will become clearer with an example. Suppose it was necessary to lie in order to save someone's life. Should you do it? Kant would reason as follows:

(1) We should do only those actions that conform to rules which we could will to be adopted universally.

(2) If you were to lie, then you would be following the rule, "It is okay to lie."

(3) This rule could not be adopted universally, because it would be self-defeating: People would stop believing one another, and then it would be impossible to lie.

(4) Therefore, you should not lie.

Although Anscombe agreed with Kant's conclusion, she was quick to point out an error in his reasoning. The difficulty arises in step (2). Why should we say that, if you lied, you would be following the rule, "It is okay to lie"? Perhaps your maxim would be "I will lie when doing so would save someone's life." *That* rule would not be self-defeating. It could become a universal law. And so, by Kant's own theory, it would be all right for you to lie. Thus, Kant's belief that lying is always wrong does not seem to be in line with his own moral theory.

2. Many of Kant's contemporaries thought that his insistence on absolute rules was strange. One reviewer challenged him with this example: Imagine that someone is fleeing from a murderer and tells you that he is going home to hide. Then the murderer comes by and asks you where the man is. You believe that if you tell the truth, you will be aiding in a murder. Furthermore, the killer is already headed the right way, so if you simply remain silent, the worst result is likely. What should you do? Let's call this the Case of the Inquiring Murderer. Under these circumstances, most of us believe that you should lie. After all, which is more important: telling the truth or saving someone's life?

Kant responded in an essay with the charmingly old-fashioned title "On a Supposed Right to Lie from Altruistic Motives," in which he gives a second argument against lying. Perhaps, he says, the man on the run has actually left his home, and by telling the truth, you would lead the killer to look in the wrong place. However, if you lie, the murderer may wander away and discover the man leaving the area, in which case you would be responsible for his death. Whoever lies, Kant says, "must answer for the consequences, however unforeseeable they were, and pay the penalty for them." Kant states his conclusion in the tone of a stern schoolmaster: "To be truthful . . . in all declarations, therefore, is a sacred and absolutely commanding decree of reason, limited by no expediency."

This argument may be stated in a general form: We are tempted to make exceptions to the rule against lying because in some cases we think that the consequences of honesty will be bad and that the consequences of lying will be good. However, we can never be certain about what the consequences will be—we cannot *know* that good results will follow. The results of lying might be unexpectedly bad. Therefore, the best policy is to avoid the known evil—lying—and let the consequences come as they may. Even if the consequences are bad, they will not be our fault, for we will have done our duty.

A similar argument would apply to Truman's decision to drop atomic bombs on Hiroshima and Nagasaki. The bombs were dropped in the hope that it would end the war. But Truman did not know that this would happen. The Japanese might have hunkered down, and the invasion might still have been necessary. So, Truman was betting hundreds of thousands of lives on the mere hope that good results might ensue.

The problems with this argument are obvious enough—so obvious, in fact, that it is surprising that a philosopher of Kant's caliber was not more sensitive to them. In the first place, the argument depends on an unreasonably pessimistic view of what we can know. Sometimes we can be quite confident of what the consequences will be, in which case we need not hesitate because of uncertainty. Moreover—and this is more significant, philosophically— Kant seems to assume that we would be morally responsible for any bad consequences of lying, but we would *not* be responsible for any bad consequences of telling the truth. Suppose, as a result of our telling the truth, the murderer found his victim and killed him. Kant seems to assume that we would be blameless. But can we escape responsibility so easily? After all, we told the murderer where to go. This argument, then, is not convincing.

Thus, Kant has failed to prove that lying is always wrong. The Case of the Inquiring Murderer shows what a tough row he chose to hoe. While Kant believes that lying "obliterates one's dignity as a human being," common sense says that some lies are harmless. In fact, we have a name for them: white lies. Aren't white lies acceptable—or even required—when they can be used to save someone's life? This points to the main difficulty for the belief in absolute rules: Shouldn't a rule be broken when following it would be disastrous?

9.4. Conflicts between Rules

Suppose it is held to be absolutely wrong to do X in any circumstances and also wrong to do Y in any circumstances. Then what about the case in which a person must choose between doing X and doing Y? This kind of conflict seems to show that moral rules can't be absolute.

Consider an example. Suppose we believe that it is always wrong both *to intentionally kill an innocent person* and *to let people suffer horribly with no compensating benefits*. Now consider a situation faced by health-care workers in New Orleans in 2005. As

Hurricane Katrina approached the city and people fled, a skeletal crew of doctors and nurses stayed behind at Memorial Medical Center in order to tend to the patients who could not be evacuated. For a day or so after the storm hit, the situation was manageable. The city lost power, but the back-up generators in the hospital came on, and the machines kept humming. Badly needed help, however, did not arrive. On day two, the generators failed, the hospital lost power, and the air grew stifling hot. "Water stopped flowing from the taps, toilets were backed up, and the stench of sewage mixed with the odor of hundreds of unwashed bodies," one reporter later wrote. On day three, the remaining doctors and nurses labored under these conditions all day long, with little to eat, and on little sleep.

At this point, the health-care workers faced a grave dilemma: either euthanize the remaining critical-care patients or let them suffer until they die. There was no third option. Conditions in the hospital were horrendous; evacuation was impossible; and many of the patients had been close to death even before the hurricane hit. So one of the "absolute" principles had to be violated: either innocent people had to be killed, or needless suffering had to occur. (In practice, investigators later came to believe that more than twenty patients had been euthanized. One doctor, Anna Pou, was arrested on four counts of second-degree murder, but eventually all the charges were dropped.)

Don't such dilemmas prove that there are no absolute moral rules? The argument is impressive but limited. It can be levied only against a *pair* of rules; two rules are needed to create the conflict. Yet there might still be just one absolute rule. For example, even given the experience in New Orleans, *never intentionally kill an innocent human being* could still be a rule that holds in all circumstances. So could, *never let people suffer horribly with no compensating benefits*. However, both rules could not be absolute. A choice had to be made.

9.5. Kant's Insight

Few contemporary philosophers would defend Kant's Categorical Imperative. Yet it might be wrong to dismiss that principle too quickly. As Alasdair MacIntyre (1929–) observes, "For many who have never heard of philosophy, let alone of Kant, morality is roughly what Kant said it was"—that is, a system of rules that one must follow from a sense of duty. Is there some basic idea underlying the Categorical Imperative that we might accept, even if we don't believe in absolute moral rules? I think there is.

Remember that Kant viewed the Categorical Imperative as binding on rational agents simply because they are rational; in other words, a person who rejected this principle would be guilty not merely of being immoral but also of being irrational. This is a compelling idea. But what exactly does it mean? In what sense would it be irrational to reject the Categorical Imperative?

Note that a moral judgment must be backed by good reasons— if it is true that you ought (or ought not) to do such-and-such, then there must be a reason why you should (or should not) do it. For example, you might think that you ought not to set forest fires because property would be destroyed and people would be killed. The Kantian twist is to point out that *if you accept any considerations as reasons in one case, then you must accept them as reasons in other cases as well.* If there is another case in which property would be destroyed and people killed, you must accept this as a reason in that case, too. It is no good saying that you can accept reasons some of the time, but not all the time, or that other people must respect them, but not you. Moral reasons, if they are valid at all, are binding on all people at all times. This is a requirement of consistency, and Kant was right to think that no rational person may deny it.

This insight has some important implications. It implies that a person cannot regard herself as special, from a moral point of view: She cannot consistently think that she is permitted to act in ways that are forbidden to others, or that her interests are more important than other people's interests. As one person put it, I cannot say that it is all right for me to drink your beer and then complain when you drink mine. If Kant was not the first to recognize this, he was the first to make it the cornerstone of a fully worked-out system of morals.

But Kant went one step further and said that consistency requires rules that have no exceptions. One can see how his insight pushed him in that direction, but the extra step was not necessary, and it causes trouble for his theory. Rules, even within a Kantian framework, need not be absolute. All that Kant's basic idea requires is that when we violate a rule, we do so for a reason that we would be willing for anyone to accept. In the Case of the Inquiring Murderer, this means that we may violate the rule against lying only if we would be willing for anyone else to lie in the same circumstances. And most of us would readily agree to that.

President Truman could also say that anyone in his position would have been justified in dropping the bomb. Thus, even if Truman was wrong, Kant's arguments do not prove it. One might say that dropping the bomb was wrong because Truman had better options. Perhaps he should have shown the Japanese the power of the bomb by dropping it onto an unpopulated area—negotiations might then have been successful. Or perhaps the Allies could have simply declared victory at that point in the war, even without a Japanese surrender. Saying *things like that*, however, is very different from saying that what Truman did violated an absolute rule.

Notes on Sources

Franklin D. Roosevelt is quoted from his communication *The President of the United States to the Governments of France, Germany, Italy, Poland and His Britannic Majesty*, September 1, 1939.

The excerpts from Truman's diary are from Robert H. Ferrell, *Off the Record: The Private Papers of Harry S. Truman* (New York: Harper and Row, 1980), pp. 55–56.

Winston Churchill is quoted from his *The Second World War*, vol. 6: *Triumph and Tragedy* (New York: Houghton Mifflin Company, 1953), p. 553.

Anscombe's pamphlets ("The Justice of the Present War Examined" and "Mr Truman's Degree") are in G. E. M. Anscombe, *Ethics, Religion and Politics: Collected Philosophical Papers*, vol. 3 (Minneapolis: University of Minnesota Press, 1981). See pp. 64, 65. Also in that volume is her "Modern Moral Philosophy," pp. 26–42 (originally published in *Philosophy* 33, no. 124 [January 1958], pp. 1–19): see p. 27 (critique of Kant) and p. 34 (examples of absolute moral rules).

On Hiroshima, see Richard Rhodes, *The Making of the Atomic Bomb* (New York: Simon and Schuster, 1986), p. 715 (birds igniting), and pp. 725–726 (dying in water).

Kant's statement of the Categorical Imperative is from his *Foundations of the Metaphysics of Morals*, translated by Lewis White Beck (Indianapolis: Bobbs-Merrill, 1959), p. 38 (2: 421).

Kant's "On a Supposed Right to Lie from Altruistic Motives" is in *Critique of Practical Reason and Other Writings in Moral Philosophy*, translated by Lewis White Beck (Chicago: University of Chicago Press, 1949). The quotations are from p. 348 (VIII, 427).

On the dilemma in New Orleans, read Sheri Fink, "The Deadly Choices at Memorial," *The New York Times*, August 25, 2009.

Alasdair MacIntyre's remark about Kant is from *A Short History of Ethics* (New York: Macmillan, 1966), p. 190.

CHAPTER **10**

*K*ant and Respect for Persons

Are there any who would not admire man?
GIOVANNI PICO DELLA MIRANDOLA,
ORATION ON THE DIGNITY OF MAN (1486)

10.1. Kant's Core Ideas

Immanuel Kant thought that human beings occupy a special place in creation. Of course, he was not alone in thinking this. From ancient times, humans have considered themselves to be essentially different from all other creatures—and not just different, but better. In fact, humans have traditionally considered themselves to be quite fabulous. Kant certainly did. On his view, human beings have "an intrinsic worth" or "dignity" that makes them valuable "above all price."

Other animals, Kant thought, have value only insofar as they serve human purposes. In his *Lectures on Ethics* (1779), Kant writes, "But so far as animals are concerned, we have no direct duties. Animals . . . are there merely as means to an end. That end is man." We may, therefore, use animals in any way we please. We don't even have a "direct duty" to refrain from torturing them. Kant did condemn the abuse of animals, but not because the animals would be hurt. He worried, rather, about us: "He who is cruel to animals also becomes hard in his dealings with men."

When Kant said that human beings are valuable "above all price," this was not mere rhetoric. Kant meant that people are irreplaceable. If a child dies, this is a tragedy, and it remains tragic even if another child is born into the same family. On the other hand, "mere things" are replaceable. If your printer breaks, then everything is fine if you can get another printer. People, Kant believed, have a "dignity" that mere things lack.

Two facts about people, Kant thought, support this judgment.

First, because people have desires, things that satisfy those desires can have value *for* people. By contrast, "mere things" have value only insofar as they promote human ends. Thus, if you want to become a better poker player, a book about poker will have value for you; but, apart from such ends, books about poker are worthless. Or, if you want to go somewhere, a car will have value for you; yet, apart from such desires, cars have no value.

Mere animals, Kant thought, are too primitive to have desires and goals. Thus, they are "mere things." Kant did not believe, for example, that milk has value *for* the cat who wishes to drink it. Today, however, we are more impressed with the mental life of animals than Kant was. We believe that nonhuman animals do have desires and goals. So, perhaps there are Kantian grounds for saying that animals are not "mere things."

Yet Kant's second reason would not apply to animals. People, Kant said, have "an intrinsic worth, i.e., dignity" because they are *rational agents*, that is, free agents capable of making their own decisions, setting their own goals, and guiding their conduct by reason. The only way that moral goodness can exist, Kant held, is for rational creatures *to act from a good will*—that is, to apprehend what they should do and act from a sense of duty. Human beings are the only rational agents that exist on earth; nonhuman animals lack free will, and they do not "guide their conduct by reason" because their rational capacities are too limited. If people disappeared, then so would the moral dimension of the world. This second fact is especially important for Kant.

Thus, Kant believed, human beings are not merely one valuable thing among others. Humans are the ones who do the valuing, and it is their conscientious actions alone that have moral worth. Human beings tower above the realm of things.

These thoughts are central to Kant's moral system. Kant believed that all of our duties can be derived from one ultimate principle, which he called the Categorical Imperative. Kant gave this principle different formulations, but at one point he put it like this:

> Act so that you treat humanity, whether in your own person or
> in that of another, always as an end and never as a means only.

Because people are so valuable, morality requires us to treat them "always as an end and never as a means only." What does this mean, and why should anyone believe it?

To treat people "as an end" means, on the most superficial level, treating them well. We must promote their welfare, respect their rights, avoid harming them, and generally "endeavor, so far as we can, to further the ends of others." But Kant's idea also has a deeper implication. To treat people as ends requires treating them with respect. Thus, we may not manipulate people or "use" people to achieve our goals, no matter how good those goals may be. Kant gives this example: Suppose you need money, and you want a loan, but you know you cannot repay it. In desperation, you consider telling your friend you will repay it in order to get the money. May you do this? Perhaps you need the money for a good purpose—so good, in fact, that you might convince yourself that a lie would be justified. Nevertheless, you should not lie to your friend. If you did, you would be manipulating her and using her "merely as a means."

On the other hand, what would it be like to treat your friend "as an end"? Suppose you tell the truth—you tell her why you need the money, and you tell her you won't be able to pay her back. Then your friend can make up her own mind about whether to give you the loan. She can consult her own values and wishes, exercise her own powers of reasoning, and make a free choice. If she then decides to give you the money for your stated purpose, she will be choosing *to make that purpose her own.* Thus, you will not be using her as a mere means to achieving your goal, for it will be her goal, too. Thus, for Kant, to treat people as ends is to treat them "as beings who [can] contain in themselves the end of the very same action."

When you tell your friend the truth, and she gives you money, you are using her as a means to getting the money. However, Kant does not object to treating someone as a means; he objects to treating someone *only* as a means. Consider another example: Suppose your bathroom sink is stopped up. Would it be okay to call in a plumber—to "use" the plumber as a means to unclogging the drain? Kant would have no problem with this, either. The plumber, after all, understands the situation. You are not deceiving or manipulating him. He may freely choose to unclog your drain in exchange for payment. Although you are treating the plumber as a means, you are also treating him with dignity, as an "end-in-himself."

Treating people as ends, and respecting their rational capacities, has other implications. We should not force adults to do things against their will; instead, we should let them make their own decisions. We should, therefore, be wary of laws that aim to protect people from themselves—for example, laws requiring people to wear seat belts or motorcycle helmets. Also, we shouldn't forget that respecting *people* requires respecting *ourselves*. I should take good care of myself; I should develop my talents; I should do more than just slide by.

Kant's moral system is not easy to grasp. To understand it better, let's consider how Kant applied his ideas to the practice of criminal punishment. The rest of this chapter is devoted to that example.

10.2. Retribution and Utility in the Theory of Punishment

Jeremy Bentham (1748–1832) said that "all punishment is mischief: all punishment in itself is evil." Bentham had a point. As a society, we punish people by making them pay fines or go to prison. Sometimes we even kill them. Punishment, by its nature, always involves inflicting harm. How can it be right to hurt people?

The traditional answer is that punishment is justified as a way of "paying back" the offender for his wicked deed. Those who have committed a crime deserve to be treated badly. It is a matter of justice: If you harm other people, justice requires that you be harmed, too. As the ancient saying has it, "An eye for an eye, and a tooth for a tooth." According to the doctrine of Retributivism, this is the main justification of punishment.

On Bentham's view, Retributivism is a wholly unsatisfactory idea, because it advocates the infliction of suffering without any compensating gain in happiness. Retributivism would have us increase, not decrease, the amount of misery in the world. Kant was a retributivist, and he openly embraced this implication. In *The Critique of Practical Reason* (1788), he writes,

> When, however, someone who delights in annoying and vexing peace-loving folk receives at last a right good beating, it is

certainly an ill, but everyone approves of it and considers it as good in itself even if nothing further results from it.

Thus, punishing people may increase the amount of misery in the world, but that is all right, because the extra suffering is borne by those who deserve it.

Utilitarianism takes a very different approach. According to Utilitarianism, our duty is to do whatever will increase the amount of happiness in the world. Punishment is, on its face, "an evil" because it makes the punished person unhappy. Thus, Bentham, a utilitarian, says, "If [punishment] ought at all to be admitted, it ought to be admitted in as far as it promises to exclude some greater evil." In other words, punishment can be justified only if it does enough good to outweigh the bad. And utilitarians have traditionally thought that it does. If someone breaks the law, then punishing that person can have several benefits.

First, punishment provides comfort and gratification to victims and their families. People feel very strongly that someone who mugged, raped, or robbed them should not go free. Victims also live in fear when they know that their attacker is still on the street. Philosophers usually ignore this justification of punishment, but it plays a prominent role in our legal system. Judges, lawyers, and juries often want to know what victims want. Indeed, whether the police will make an arrest, and whether the district attorney's office will prosecute a case, often depends on the wishes of the victims.

Second, by locking up criminals, or by executing them, we take them off the street. With fewer criminals on the loose, there is less crime. In this way, prisons protect society and thus reduce unhappiness. Of course, this justification does not apply to punishments in which the offender remains free, such as when a criminal is sentenced to probation with community service.

Third, punishment reduces crime by deterring would-be criminals. Someone who is tempted to commit a crime might not do so if he knows he might be punished. Obviously, the threat of punishment is not always effective; sometimes people break the law anyway. But there will be *less* misconduct if punishments are threatened. Imagine what would happen if the police stopped arresting thieves;

surely there would be a lot more theft. Deterring crime thus prevents unhappiness.

Fourth, a well-designed system of punishment might help to rehabilitate wrongdoers. Criminals often have mental and emotional problems. Many are uneducated and illiterate and cannot hold down jobs. Why not respond to crime by attacking the problems that cause it? If someone is dangerous, we may imprison him. But while we have him behind bars, why not address his problems with psychological therapy, educational opportunities, and job training? If one day he can return to society as a productive citizen, then both he and society will benefit.

In America, the utilitarian view of punishment was once dominant. In 1954, the American Prison Association changed its name to "the American Correctional Association" and encouraged prisons to become "correctional facilities." Prisons were thus asked to "correct" inmates, not to "punish" them. Prison reform was common in the 1950s and 1960s. Prisons offered their inmates drug treatment programs, vocational training classes, and group counseling sessions, hoping to turn them into good citizens.

Those days, however, are long gone. The United States took a sharp retributivist turn in the 1970s, increasing the average length of prison sentences and locking up more drug offenders. This resulted in vastly more prisoners at any given time. Today the United States houses around 2.3 million inmates, giving it the highest incarceration rate in the world. Most of those inmates are in state prisons, not federal prisons, and the states that must operate those facilities are strapped for cash. As a result, most of the programs aimed at rehabilitation were either scaled back or eliminated. The rehabilitation mentality of the 1960s has thus been replaced by a warehousing mentality, marked by prison overcrowding and plagued by underfunding. This new reality, which is less pleasant for the inmates themselves, suggests a victory for Retributivism.

10.3. Kant's Retributivism

The utilitarian theory of punishment has many opponents. Some critics say that prison reform does not work. California had the most vigorous program of reform in the United States, yet its prisoners were especially likely to commit crimes after being released. Most of the opposition, however, is based on theoretical considerations that go back at least to Kant.

Kant despised "the serpent-windings of Utilitarianism" because, he said, the theory is incompatible with human dignity. In the first place, it has us calculating how to use people as means to our ends. If we imprison the criminal in order to keep society safe, we are merely using him for the benefit of others. This violates Kant's belief that "one man ought never to be dealt with merely as a means subservient to the purpose of another."

Moreover, rehabilitation is really just the attempt to mold people into what *we* want them to be. As such, it violates their right to decide for themselves what sort of people they will be. We do have the right to respond to their wickedness by "paying them back" for it, but we do not have the right to violate their integrity by trying to manipulate their personalities.

Thus, Kant would have no part of utilitarian justifications. Instead, he believes that punishment should be governed by two principles. First, people should be punished simply because they have committed crimes, and for no other reason. Second, punishment should be *proportionate* to the seriousness of the crime. Small punishments may suffice for small crimes, but big punishments are necessary for big crimes:

> But what is the mode and measure of punishment which public justice takes as its principle and standard? It is just the principle of equality, by which the pointer of the scale of justice is made to incline no more to the one side than to the other. . . . Hence it may be said: "If you slander another, you slander yourself; if you steal from another, you steal from yourself; if you strike another, you strike yourself; if you kill another, you kill yourself." This is . . . the only principle which . . . can definitely assign both the quality and the quantity of a just penalty.

Kant's second principle leads him to endorse capital punishment; for in response to murder, only death is appropriate. In a famous passage, Kant says:

> Even if a civil society resolved to dissolve itself with the consent of all its members—as might be supposed in the case of a

people inhabiting an island resolving to separate and scatter throughout the whole world—the last murderer lying in prison ought to be executed before the resolution was carried out. This ought to be done in order that everyone may realize the desert of his deeds, and that blood-guiltiness may not remain on the people; for otherwise they will all be regarded as participants in the murder. . . .

Although a Kantian must support the death penalty *in theory*, she might oppose it *in practice*. The worry, in practice, is that innocent people might be killed by mistake. In the United States, around 130 death row inmates have been released from prison after being proved innocent. None of those people were actually killed. But with so many close calls, it is almost certain that some innocent people have been put to death—and advocates of reform point to specific, troubling cases. Thus, in deciding whether to support a policy of capital punishment, Kantians must balance the injustice of the occasional, deadly mistake against the injustice of letting killers live.

Kant's principles describe a general theory of punishment: Wrongdoers must be punished, and the punishment must fit the crime. This theory is deeply opposed to the Christian idea of turning the other cheek. In the Sermon on the Mount, Jesus avows, "You have heard that it was said, 'An eye for an eye and a tooth for a tooth.' But I say to you, Do not resist the one who is evil. If anyone slaps you on the right cheek, turn to him the other also." For Kant, such a response to evil is not only imprudent, but unjust.

What arguments can be given for Kant's Retributivism? As we noted, Kant regards punishment as a matter of justice. He says that justice is not done if the guilty go unpunished. That is one argument. Also, we discussed why Kant rejects the utilitarian view of punishment. But he also gives another argument, based on his idea of treating people as "ends-in-themselves."

How does this argument go? On the face of it, it seems unlikely that we could describe punishing someone as "respecting him as a person" or as "treating him as an end." How could sending someone to prison be a way of respecting him? Even more paradoxically, how could executing someone be a way of treating him with dignity?

For Kant, treating someone "as an end" means treating him as a rational being, who is responsible for his behavior. So now we may ask: What does it mean to be a responsible being?

Let's first consider what it means *not* to be such a being. Mere animals, who lack reason, are not responsible for their actions; nor are people who are mentally ill and cannot control themselves. In such cases, it would be absurd to "hold them accountable." We could not properly feel gratitude or resentment toward them, because they are not responsible for any good or ill they cause. Moreover, we cannot expect them to understand *why* we treat them as we do, any more than they understand why they behave as they do. So we have no choice but to deal with them by manipulating them. When we scold a dog for eating off the table, for example, we are merely trying to "train" him.

On the other hand, a rational being can freely decide what to do, based on his own conception of what is best. Rational beings *are* responsible for their behavior, and so they are accountable for what they do. We may feel gratitude when they behave well and resentment when they behave badly. Reward and punishment—not "training" or other forms of manipulation—are the natural expressions of gratitude and resentment. Thus, in punishing people, we are holding them responsible for their actions in a way in which we cannot hold mere animals responsible. We are responding to them not as people who are "sick" or who have no control over themselves, but as people who have freely chosen their evil deeds.

Furthermore, in dealing with responsible agents, we may properly allow their conduct to determine, at least in part, how we respond to them. If someone has been kind to you, you may respond by being generous; and if someone is nasty to you, then you may take that into account in deciding how to respond. And why shouldn't you? Why should you treat everyone alike, regardless of how *they* have chosen to behave?

Kant gives this last point a distinctive twist. There is, on his view, a deep reason for responding to other people "in kind." When we choose to do something, after consulting our own values, we are in effect saying *this is the sort of thing that should be done*. In Kant's terminology, we are implying that our conduct be made into a "universal law." Therefore, when a rational being decides to treat people in a certain way, he decrees that *this is the way people are to be treated.* Thus, if we treat him the same way in return, we are doing nothing more than treating him *as he has decided that people are to be treated.* If he treats others badly, and we treat him badly, we are complying with his own decision. We are, in a perfectly clear sense, respecting him by allowing his own judgment to control how we treat him. Of the criminal, Kant says, "His own evil deed draws the punishment upon himself."

This last argument can be questioned. Why should we adopt the criminal's principle of action, rather than our own? Shouldn't we try to "be better than he is"? Also, bear in mind that even the wicked sometimes behave well. So if we treat the evildoer well, wouldn't we also be following his judgment—a judgment that he has endorsed on many occasions?

At the end of the day, what we think of Kant's theory may depend on our view of criminal behavior. If we see criminals as victims of circumstance, who do not ultimately control their own lives, then the utilitarian model will appeal to us. On the other hand, if we see criminals as rational agents who freely choose to do harm, then Kantian Retributivism will have more appeal. The resolution of this great debate about punishment might thus turn on whether we believe that human beings have free will or whether we believe that outside forces impact human behavior so deeply that our freedom is an illusion. The debate about free will, however, is so complex, and so concerned with matters outside of ethics, that we will not discuss it here. This kind of dialectical situation is common in philosophy: When you study one matter deeply, you often come to realize that it depends on something else—something that is just as hard as the problem you began with.

Notes on Sources

Kant's remarks on animals are from his *Lectures on Ethics*, translated by Louis Infield (New York: Harper and Row, 1963), pp. 239–240. I altered the second quotation without changing its meaning: "he who is cruel to animals also becomes hard in his dealings with men" (instead of "becomes hard also").

The Categorical Imperative is formulated in terms of treating persons as ends in *Foundations of the Metaphysics of Morals*, translated by Lewis

White Beck (Indianapolis: Bobbs-Merrill, 1959), p. 46 (2: 429). Kant's remarks about "dignity" and "price" are on pp. 51–52 (2: 434–435).

Bentham's statement "All punishment is mischief" is from *The Principles of Morals and Legislation* (New York: Hafner, 1948), p. 170.

Kant is quoted on punishment from *The Metaphysical Elements of Justice*, translated by John Ladd (Indianapolis: Bobbs-Merrill, 1965), pp. 99–107, except that the "right good beating" quote is from *Critique of Practical Reason*, translated by Lewis White Beck (Chicago: University of Chicago Press, 1949), p. 170 (V, 61).

On the change from "prisons" to "correctional facilities," see Blake McKelvey, *American Prisons: A History of Good Intentions* (Montclair, NJ: Patterson Smith, 1977), p. 357. On changes in American corrections between the 1960s and 1990s, see Eric Schlosser, "The Prison-Industrial Complex," *Atlantic Monthly*, December 1998.

On incarceration rates in the U.S. and elsewhere, see the Prison Policy Initiative's "Mass Incarceration: The Whole Pie 2017" and "States of Incarceration: The Global Context 2016," both at prisonpolicy.org.

On December 22, 2006, a story on National Public Radio cited California officials as saying that California has the highest recidivism rate in the country.

Jesus talks about "turning the other cheek" in Matthew 5:38–39. I have used the English Standard Version translation of *The Holy Bible* (2001).

CHAPTER 11

Feminism and the Ethics of Care

But it is obvious that the values of women differ very often from the values which have been made by the other sex; naturally, this is so. Yet it is the masculine values that prevail.

VIRGINIA WOOLF, *A ROOM OF ONE'S OWN* (1929)

11.1. Do Women and Men Think Differently about Ethics?

The idea that women and men think differently has traditionally been used to insult or belittle women. Aristotle said that women are less rational than men, and so men naturally rule them. Immanuel Kant agreed, adding that women "lack civil personality" and should have no voice in public life. Jean-Jacques Rousseau tried to put a good face on this by emphasizing that women and men merely possess different virtues; but, of course, it turns out that men's virtues fit them for leadership, whereas women's virtues fit them for home and hearth.

Against this background, it is not surprising that the women's movement of the 1960s and 1970s denied that women and men differ psychologically. The conception of men as rational and women as emotional was dismissed by feminists as a mere stereotype. Nature makes no mental or moral distinction between the sexes, it was said; and when there seem to be differences, it is only because women have been conditioned by an oppressive society to behave in "feminine" ways.

These days, however, most feminists believe that women do think differently than men. But they also believe that women's ways are not inferior. On the contrary, female ways of thinking yield insights that have been missed in male-dominated areas. Thus, by attending to the distinctive approach of women, we can make progress in subjects that seem stalled. Ethics is said to be a leading candidate for this treatment.

Kohlberg's Stages of Moral Development. Consider the following dilemma, devised by the educational psychologist Lawrence Kohlberg (1927–1987). Heinz's wife is near death, and her only hope is a drug that was discovered by a pharmacist who is now selling it for an outrageously high price. The drug costs $200 to make, and the pharmacist is selling it for $2,000. Heinz can raise $1,000, but the pharmacist told him that half wasn't enough. When Heinz promised to pay the rest later, the pharmacist still refused. In desperation, Heinz considers stealing the drug. Would that be wrong?

This problem, known as "Heinz's Dilemma," was used by Kohlberg in studying the moral development of children. Kohlberg interviewed children of various ages, presenting them with a series of dilemmas and asking them questions designed to reveal their thinking. Analyzing their responses, Kohlberg concluded that there are six stages of moral development. In these stages, the individual conceives of "right" in terms of

> obeying authority and avoiding punishment (stage 1);
>
> satisfying one's own desires and letting others do the same, through fair exchanges (stage 2);
>
> cultivating one's relationships and performing the duties appropriate to one's social roles (stage 3);
>
> obeying the law and maintaining the welfare of the group (stage 4);
>
> upholding the basic rights and values of one's society (stage 5);
>
> abiding by abstract, universal moral principles (stage 6).

So, if all goes well, we begin life with a self-centered desire to avoid punishment, and we end life with a commitment to a set of abstract moral principles. Kohlberg, however, believed that few adults make it to stage 5, much less to stage 6.

Heinz's Dilemma was presented to an 11-year-old boy named Jake, who thought it was obvious that Heinz should steal the drug. Jake explained,

> For one thing, a human life is worth more than money, and if the druggist only makes $1,000, he is still going to live, but if Heinz doesn't steal the drug, his wife is going to die.
> *(Why is life worth more than money?)*
> Because the druggist can get a thousand dollars later from rich people with cancer, but Heinz can't get his wife again.
> *(Why not?)*
> Because people are all different and so you couldn't get Heinz's wife again.

But Amy, also 11, saw the matter differently. Should Heinz steal the drug? Compared to Jake, Amy seems hesitant and evasive:

> Well, I don't think so. I think there might be other ways besides stealing it, like if he could borrow the money or make a loan or something, but he really shouldn't steal the drug— but his wife shouldn't die either. . . . If he stole the drug, he might save his wife then, but if he did, he might have to go to jail, and then his wife might get sicker again, and he couldn't get more of the drug, and it might not be good. So, they should really just talk it out and find some other way to make the money.

The interviewer asks Amy further questions, but she will not budge; she refuses to accept the terms in which the problem is posed. Instead, she recasts the issue as a conflict between Heinz and the pharmacist that must be resolved by further discussions.

In terms of Kohlberg's stages, Jake seems to have advanced beyond Amy. Amy's response is typical of people operating at stage 3, where personal relationships are paramount—Heinz and the pharmacist must work things out between them. Jake, on the other hand, appeals to impersonal principles—"a human life is worth more than money." Jake seems to be operating at one of the later stages.

Gilligan's Objection. Kohlberg began studying moral development in the 1950s. Back then, psychologists almost always studied behavior rather than thought processes, and psychological researchers were thought of as men in white coats who watched rats run through mazes. Kohlberg's humanistic, cognitive approach was more appealing. However, his central idea was flawed. It is legitimate to study how people think at different ages—if children think differently at ages 5, 10, and 15, then that is certainly worth knowing about. It is also worthwhile to identify the best ways of thinking. But these projects are different. One involves observing how children, in fact, think; the other involves assessing ways of thinking as better or worse. Different kinds of evidence are relevant to each investigation, and there is no reason to assume in advance that the results will match. Contrary to what older people think, age might not bring wisdom.

Kohlberg's theory has also been criticized from a feminist perspective. In 1982, Carol Gilligan wrote a book called *In a Different Voice*, in which she objects to what Kohlberg says about Jake and Amy. These children think differently, she says, but Amy's way is not inferior. When confronted with Heinz's Dilemma, Amy responds to the personal aspects of the situation, as females typically do, whereas Jake, thinking like a male, sees only "a conflict between life and property that can be resolved by a logical deduction." Jake's response will be judged "at a higher level" only if one assumes, as Kohlberg does, that an ethic of principle is superior to an ethic of intimacy and caring. But why should we assume that? Admittedly, most moral philosophers have favored an ethic of principle, but most moral philosophers have been men.

The "male way of thinking"—the appeal to impersonal principles— abstracts away all the details that give each situation its special flavor. Women, Gilligan says, find it harder to ignore those details. Amy worries, "If [Heinz] stole the drug, he might save his wife then, but if he did, he might have to go to jail, and then his wife might get sicker again, and he couldn't get more of the drug." Jake, who reduces the situation to "a human life is worth more than money," ignores all this.

Gilligan suggests that women's basic moral orientation is one of caring. Sensitivity to the needs of others leads women to "attend to voices other than their own and to include in their judgment other points of view." Thus, Amy could not simply reject the pharmacist's point of view; rather, she wanted to talk to him and try to accommodate him. According to Gilligan, "Women's moral weakness, manifest in an apparent diffusion and confusion of judgment, is thus inseparable from women's moral strength, an overriding concern with relationships and responsibilities."

Other feminists have taken these ideas and molded them into a distinctive view of ethics. Virginia Held (1929-) sums up the central idea: "Caring, empathy, feeling with others, being sensitive to each other's feelings, all may be better guides to what morality requires in actual contexts than may abstract rules of reason, or rational calculation, or at least they may be necessary components of an adequate morality."

Before discussing this idea, we may pause to consider how "feminine" it really is. *Do* women and men think differently about ethics? And if they do, why do they?

Do Women and Men Think Differently? Since Gilligan's book appeared, psychologists have conducted hundreds of studies on gender, the emotions, and morality. These studies reveal some differences between women and men. Women tend to score higher than men on tests that measure empathy. Also, brain scans reveal that women have a lower tendency to enjoy seeing people punished who have treated them unfairly—perhaps because women empathize even with those who have wronged them. Finally, women seem to care more about close personal relationships, whereas men care more about larger networks of shallow relationships. As Roy Baumeister put it, "Women specialize in the narrow sphere of intimate relationships. Men specialize in the larger group."

Women and men probably do think differently about ethics. These differences, however, cannot be very great. It is not as though women make judgments that men cannot understand, or vice versa. Men know the value of caring relationships, even if they have to be reminded sometimes; and they can agree with Amy that the happiest solution to Heinz's Dilemma would be for the husband and the pharmacist to work it out. For their part, women will hardly disagree that human life is worth more than money. And when we look at individuals, we find that some men are especially caring, while some women rely heavily on abstract principles. Plainly, the two sexes do not inhabit different moral universes. One scholarly article reviewed 180 studies and found that women are only slightly more care-oriented than men, and men are only slightly more justice-oriented than women. Even this watered-down conclusion, however, invites the question: Why should women be, on average, more caring than men?

We might look for a social explanation. Perhaps women care more because of the social roles they occupy. Traditionally, women have been expected to do the housework and to take care of the kids. Even if this expectation is sexist, the fact remains that women have often fulfilled these functions. And it is easy to see how taking care of a family could instill an ethic of caring into someone. Thus, the care perspective could be part of the psychological conditioning that girls receive.

We might also seek a genetic explanation. Some differences between males and females show up at a very early age. One-year-old girls will spend more time looking at a film of a face than a film of cars, whereas one-year-old boys prefer the cars. Even one-*day*-old girls (but not the boys!) will spend more time looking at a friendly face than looking at a mechanical object of the same size. This suggests that females might naturally be more social than males. If this were true, why would it be true?

Charles Darwin's theory of evolution might provide some insight. We may think of the Darwinian "struggle for survival" as a competition to get the maximum number of one's genes into the next generation. Traits that help accomplish this will be preserved in future generations, while traits that work against this will tend to disappear. In the 1970s, researchers in the new field of Evolutionary Psychology (then called "Sociobiology") began to apply these ideas to the study of human nature. The idea is that people today have the emotions and behavioral tendencies that enabled their ancestors to survive and reproduce in high numbers.

From this point of view, the key difference between males and females is that men can father thousands of children, while women can give birth only once every nine and a half months, until menopause. This means that males and females have evolved different reproductive strategies. For men, the optimum strategy is to impregnate as many women as possible. Thus, the man will spend his energy on finding new partners rather than on helping to raise his own children. For women, the optimum strategy is to invest heavily in each child and to have sex only with men who will stick around. This might explain why men have a higher sex drive than women. But also, it might explain why men and women have different attitudes toward relationships in general. In particular, it might explain why women are more attracted to the values of the nuclear family—including the value of caring.

This kind of explanation is often misunderstood. The point is not that people consciously calculate how to propagate their genes; no one does that. Evolution may shape our desires, but it doesn't micromanage our thought processes. Nor is the point that people *should* calculate in this way; from an ethical point of view, we should not. The point is just to explain what we observe.

11.2. Implications for Moral Judgment

The ethics of care is closely identified with modern feminist philosophy. As Annette Baier (1929–2012) put it, "'Care' is the new buzzword." However, one need not embrace an ethic of care in order to be a feminist. Many feminists—men as well as women—are simply people who wish to understand and correct ongoing injustices against women. For example, a feminist may want to understand why women in America get paid less than men. Why did the average female working full-time in 2015 make $40,742, while the average male made $51,212? Being concerned about such a thing doesn't imply belief in an ethic of care. However, we will focus on that ethic because it may represent an alternative to such theories as Utilitarianism and the Social Contract Theory.

One way of understanding an ethical view is to ask what difference it would make in practice. Does an ethic of care have different implications than a "male" approach to ethics? Let's consider three examples.

Family and Friends. Traditional theories of obligation are notoriously ill-suited to describing life among family and friends. Those theories take the notion of *what we should do* as morally fundamental.

But, as Baier observes, when we try to construe "being a loving parent" as a duty, we encounter problems. A loving parent is motivated by love, not by duty. If parents care for their children only because they feel it is their duty, their children will sense it and realize they are unloved.

Moreover, the ideas of equality and impartiality that pervade theories of obligation seem deeply antagonistic to the values of love and friendship. John Stuart Mill (1806–1873) said that a moral agent must be "as strictly impartial as a disinterested and benevolent spectator." But that is not the standpoint of a parent or a friend. We do not regard our family and friends as mere members of the great crowd of humanity; we think of them as special.

The ethics of care, on the other hand, is perfectly suited to describe such relations. The ethics of care does not take "obligation" or "duty" as fundamental; nor does it require that we impartially promote the interests of everyone alike. Instead, it begins with a conception of moral life as a network of relationships with specific people, and it sees "living well" as caring for those people, attending to their needs, and maintaining their trust.

These outlooks lead to different judgments about what we may do. May I devote my time and resources to caring for my friends and family, even if this means ignoring the needs of other people? From an impartial point of view, I should not ignore the needs of strangers; I should promote the interests of everyone alike. But few of us accept that view. The ethics of care affirms the priority that we naturally give to our family and friends, and so it seems more plausible than an ethic of principle. Of course, it is not surprising that the ethics of care appears to do a good job of explaining the nature of our moral relations with friends and family. After all, those relationships are its primary inspiration.

Children with HIV. Around the world, over two million children under the age of 15 have HIV, the virus that can lead to AIDS. Half of these children receive no medical treatment. Organizations such as UNICEF could do more for these children if they had more money. By contributing to their work, we could save lives.

A traditional ethic of principle, such as Utilitarianism, would conclude from this that we have a substantial duty to support

UNICEF. The reasoning is straightforward: Almost all of us spend money on luxuries. Luxuries are not as important as protecting children from AIDS. Therefore, we should give at least some of our money to UNICEF. Of course, this argument would become complicated if we tried to fill in all the details. But the basic idea is clear enough.

One might think that an ethic of care would reach a similar conclusion—after all, shouldn't we care for those disadvantaged children? But that's not how the theory works. An ethic of care focuses on small-scale, personal relationships. If there is no such relationship, "caring" cannot take place. Nel Noddings (1929–) explains that the caring relation can exist only if the "cared-for" can interact with the "one-caring." At a minimum, the cared-for must be able to receive and acknowledge the care in a personal, one-to-one encounter. Otherwise, there is no obligation: "We are not obliged to act as one-caring if there is no possibility of completion in the other." Thus, Noddings concludes that we have no obligation to help "the needy in the far regions of the earth."

Many feminists regard Noddings's view as too extreme. Making personal relationships the whole of ethics seems as wrong-headed as ignoring them altogether. A better approach might be to say that the ethical life includes both caring relationships *and* a benevolent concern for people generally. Our obligation to support UNICEF might then be seen as arising from our obligations of benevolence. If we take this approach, we may interpret the ethics of care as *supplementing* traditional theories rather than replacing them. Annette Baier seems to have this in mind when she writes that, eventually, "women theorists will need to connect their ethics of love with what has been the men theorists' preoccupation, namely, obligation."

Animals. Do we have obligations to nonhuman animals? Should we, for example, refrain from eating them? One argument from an ethic of principle says that how we raise animals for food causes them great suffering, and so we should nourish ourselves without the cruelty. Since the modern animal rights movement began in the 1970s, this sort of argument has persuaded many people to become vegetarians.

Noddings suggests that this is a good issue "to test the basic notions on which an ethic of caring rests." What are those basic notions? First, such an ethic appeals to intuition and feeling rather than to principle. This leads to a different conclusion about vegetarianism, for most people do not feel that eating meat is wrong or that the suffering of livestock is important. Noddings observes that our emotional responses to humans are different from our responses to animals.

A second "basic notion on which an ethic of caring rests" is the primacy of personal relationships. These relationships, as we have noted, always involve the cared-for interacting with the one-caring. Noddings believes that people do have this sort of relationship with their pets:

> When one is familiar with a particular animal family, one comes to recognize its characteristic form of address. Cats, for example, lift their heads and stretch toward the one they are addressing. . . . When I enter my kitchen in the morning and my cat greets me from her favorite spot on the counter, I understand her request. This is the spot where she sits and "speaks" in her squeaky attempt to communicate her desire for a dish of milk.

A relationship is established, and the attitude of care must be summoned. But one has no such relationship with the cow in the overcrowded shed, and so, Noddings concludes, we have no obligation not to eat it.

What are we to make of this? If we use this issue "to test the basic notions on which an ethic of caring rests," does the ethic pass or fail the test? The opposing arguments are impressive. First, intuition and feeling are not reliable guides—at one time, people's intuitions told them that slavery was acceptable and that the subordination of women to men was God's plan. And second, whether the animal is in a position to respond "personally" to you may have a lot to do with the satisfaction you get from helping, but it has nothing to do with the animal's needs. Similarly, whether a faraway child would suffer from being HIV+ has nothing to do with whether she can thank you personally for helping her avoid infection. These arguments, of course, appeal to principles that are said to be typical of male reasoning. Therefore, if the ethic of care is taken to be the whole of morality, such arguments will be ignored. On the other hand, if caring is only one part of morality, the arguments from principle will have considerable force. Livestock might come within the sphere of moral concern, not because of our caring relation with them, but because of our opposition to suffering and cruelty.

11.3. Implications for Ethical Theory

It is easy to see the influence of men's experience in the ethical theories they have created. Historically, men have dominated public life, where relationships are often impersonal and contractual. In politics and business, relationships can even be adversarial when interests collide. So we negotiate; we bargain and make deals. Moreover, in public life our decisions might affect large numbers of people we do not know. So we may try to calculate which decisions will have the best overall outcome. And what do men's theories emphasize? Impersonal duty, contracts, the balancing of competing interests, and the calculation of costs and benefits.

Little wonder, then, that feminists accuse moral philosophy of having a male bias. The concerns of private life are almost wholly absent, and the "different voice" of which Carol Gilligan speaks is silent. A moral theory tailored to women's concerns would look very different. In the small-scale world of friends and family, bargaining and calculating play a much smaller role, while love and caring dominate. Once this point is made, there is no denying that morality must find a place for it.

Private life, however, is not easy to accommodate within traditional theories. As we noted, "being a loving parent" is not about calculating how one should behave. The same might be said about being a loyal friend or a dependable coworker. To be loving, loyal, and dependable is to be *a certain kind of person*, which is very different from impartially "doing your duty."

The contrast between "being a certain kind of person" and "doing your duty" lies at the heart of a larger conflict between two kinds of ethical theory. According to Virtue Ethics, to be moral is to have certain traits of character: being kind, generous, courageous, just, prudent, and so on. Theories of obligation, on the other hand, emphasize impartial duty: They portray the moral agent as someone who listens to reason, figures out the right thing to do, and does it. One of the chief arguments for Virtue Ethics is that it seems well suited to accommodate the values of both public and private life. The two spheres simply require different virtues. Public life requires justice and beneficence, while private life requires love and caring.

The ethics of care may, therefore, be seen as one part of the ethics of virtue. Many feminist philosophers view it in this light. Although Virtue Ethics is not exclusively a feminist project, it is so closely tied to feminist ideas that Annette Baier dubs its male promoters "honorary women." The verdict on the ethics of care may ultimately depend on the viability of a broader theory of the virtues.

Notes on Sources

Lawrence Kohlberg, *Essays on Moral Development*, vol. 1: *The Philosophy of Moral Development* (New York: Harper and Row, 1981). On Heinz's Dilemma: p. 12; on the six stages of moral development: pp. 409–412.

Carol Gilligan on Amy and Jake: *In a Different Voice: Psychological Theory and Women's Development* (Cambridge, MA: Harvard University Press, 1982), pp. 26, 28. The other Gilligan quotations are from pp. 16–17, 31.

Virginia Held is quoted from her "Feminist Transformations of Moral Theory," *Philosophy and Phenomenological Research* 50 (1990), p. 344.

Women score higher than men on empathy tests: M. H. Davis, "Measuring Individual Differences in Empathy: Evidence for a Multidimensional Approach," *Journal of Personality and Social Psychology* 44, no. 1 (January 1983), pp. 113–126; and P. E. Jose, "The Role of Gender and Gender Role Similarity in Readers' Identification with Story Characters," *Sex Roles* 21, nos. 9–10 (November 1989), pp. 697–713.

Brain scans and punishment: Tania Singer et al., "Empathetic Neural Responses Are Modulated by the Perceived Fairness of Others," *Nature*, January 26, 2006, pp. 466–469.

Roy F. Baumeister, "Is There Anything Good about Men?" American Psychological Association, invited address, 2007 (quotation on p. 9).

Women are only slightly more care-oriented than men: Sara Jaffee and Janet Shibley Hyde, "Gender Differences in Moral Orientation: A Meta-Analysis," *Psychological Bulletin* 126, no. 5 (2000), pp. 703–726.

Male/female differences appear at an early age: Larry Cahill, "His Brain, Her Brain," *Scientific American*, April 25, 2005 (8 pages), citing Simon Baron-Cohen and Svetlana Lutchmaya.

See *The Simple Truth about the Gender Pay Gap, Spring 2017 Edition*, released by the American Association of University Women, at aauw.org.

Annette Baier, *Moral Prejudices* (Cambridge, MA: Harvard University Press, 1994): "'Care' is the new buzzword" (p. 19); "connect their ethics of love" (p. 4); and "honorary women" (p. 2).

On children with HIV, see UNICEF's "For Every Child, End AIDS: Seventh Stocktaking Report, 2016" at unicef.org ("HIV/AIDS"/"Global and Regional Trends").

Nel Noddings is quoted from *Caring: A Feminine Approach to Ethics and Moral Education* (Berkeley: University of California Press, 1984), pp. 149–155.

CHAPTER 12

Virtue Ethics

The excellency of hogs is fatness, of men virtue.
BENJAMIN FRANKLIN, *POOR RICHARD'S ALMANACK* (1736)

12.1. The Ethics of Virtue and the Ethics of Right Action

In thinking about any subject, how you approach that subject matters mightily. What exactly are you hoping to learn? What questions do you want answered? When the great ancient philosopher, Aristotle, thought about ethics, he thought mostly about *character*. In the *Nicomachean Ethics* (ca. 325 B.C.), Aristotle asks, "What is the good of man?" and answers, "an activity of the soul in conformity with virtue." From there, Aristotle goes on to discuss such virtues as courage, self-control, generosity, and truthfulness. Thus he approached the subject of ethics by asking, *What traits of character make someone a good person?* This approach was popular in the ancient world.

As time passed, however, this way of thinking became neglected. With the coming of Christianity, a new set of ideas emerged. The Christians, like the Jews, viewed God as a lawgiver, and so they saw obedience to those laws as the key to righteous living. For the Greeks, the life of virtue was inseparable from the life of reason. But Saint Augustine, the influential fourth-century Christian thinker, distrusted reason and believed that moral goodness depends on subordinating oneself to the will of God. Thus, when medieval philosophers discussed the virtues, it was in the context of Divine Law, and the "theological virtues" of faith, hope, charity, and obedience occupied the spotlight.

After the Renaissance period (1400–1650), moral philosophy again became more secular, but philosophers did not return to the Greek way of thinking. Instead, the Divine Law was replaced with something called the "Moral Law." The Moral Law, which was said to spring from human reason rather than from God, was a system of rules specifying which actions are right. Thus, modern moral philosophers approached their subject by asking a question fundamentally different from the one asked by the ancients. Instead of asking *What traits of character make someone a good person?* they asked *What is the right thing to do?* This led them down a different path. They went on to develop theories, not of virtue, but of rightness and obligation:

- *Ethical Egoism:* Each person ought to do whatever will best promote his or her own interests.
- *The Social Contract Theory:* The right thing to do is to follow the rules that rational, self-interested people would agree to follow for their mutual benefit.
- *Utilitarianism:* One ought to do whatever will lead to the most happiness.
- *Kant's theory:* Our duty is to follow those rules that we could accept as universal laws—that is, rules that we would be willing for everyone to follow in all circumstances.

And these are the theories that have dominated moral philosophy from the 17th century on.

Should We Return to Virtue Ethics? Recently, however, some philosophers have advanced a radical idea: that we should return to Aristotle's way of thinking.

This was suggested by Elizabeth Anscombe in her article "Modern Moral Philosophy" (1958). Anscombe sees modern moral philosophy as misguided because it rests on the incoherent notion of a "law without a lawgiver." The very concepts of obligation, duty, and rightness, she says, are inseparable from this self-contradictory notion. Therefore, we should stop thinking about obligation, duty, and rightness, and return to Aristotle's approach. The virtues should once again take center stage.

In the wake of Anscombe's article, a flood of books and essays appeared discussing the virtues, and Virtue Ethics soon became a major option again. In what follows, we will first consider what Virtue Ethics is like. Then we will examine some reasons for preferring this theory to other, more modern ideas. Finally, we will consider whether we should return to Virtue Ethics.

12.2. The Virtues

A theory of virtue should have several components: a statement of what a virtue is, a list of the virtues, an account of what these virtues consist in, and an explanation of why these qualities are good. In addition, the theory should tell us whether the virtues are the same for all people or whether they differ from person to person or from culture to culture.

What Is a Virtue? Aristotle said that a virtue is a trait of character manifested in habitual action. The word "habitual" is important. The virtue of honesty, for example, is not possessed by someone who tells the truth only occasionally or only when it benefits her. The honest person is truthful as a matter of course; her actions "spring from a firm and unchangeable character."

Yet this does not distinguish virtues from vices, for vices are also traits of character manifested in habitual action. The other part of the definition is evaluative: Virtues are good, whereas vices are bad. Thus, a virtue is a *commendable* trait of character manifested in habitual action. So far, of course, we haven't been told which traits of character are good and which are bad. Later we will discuss the ways in which some particular traits are good.

For now, we may note that virtuous qualities are qualities that should normally attract us, whereas vices are qualities that should normally repel us. As Edmund L. Pincoffs (1919–1991) put it, "Some sorts of persons we prefer; others we avoid. The properties on our list [of virtues and vices] can serve as reasons for preference or avoidance."

We seek out people for different purposes, and this affects which qualities are relevant. In looking for an auto mechanic, we want someone who is skillful, honest, and conscientious; in looking for a teacher, we want someone who is knowledgeable, articulate, and patient. Thus, the virtues of auto repair are different from the virtues of teaching. But we also assess people *as people*, in a more general way, and so we also have the concept of a good person. The moral virtues are the virtues of persons as such. Thus, we may define a moral virtue as *a trait of character, manifested in habitual action, that it is good for anyone to have.*

What Are the Virtues? What, then, are the virtues? Which traits of character should be fostered in human beings? There is no short answer, but the following is a partial list:

benevolence	fairness	prudence
civility	friendliness	reasonableness
compassion	generosity	resourcefulness
conscientiousness	honesty	self-discipline
cooperativeness	justice	self-reliance
courage	loyalty	tactfulness
dependability	moderation	thoughtfulness
diligence	patience	tolerance

This list could be expanded, of course.

What Do These Virtues Consist In? It is one thing to say, in general, that we should be conscientious, compassionate, and tolerant; it is another thing to say exactly what these character traits are. Each virtue has its own distinctive features and raises its own distinctive problems. Let's consider four examples.

1. *Courage.* According to Aristotle, virtues are midpoints between extremes: A virtue is "the mean by reference to two vices: the one of excess and the other of deficiency." Courage is a mean between the extremes of cowardice and foolhardiness—it is cowardly to run away from all danger, yet it is foolhardy to risk too much.

Courage is sometimes said to be a military virtue because soldiers obviously need to have it. But not only soldiers need courage. We all need it, and not just when we face a preexisting danger, such as an enemy soldier or a grizzly bear. Sometimes we need the courage to *create* a situation that will be unpleasant for us. Here are some examples. It takes courage to apologize. It takes courage to volunteer to do something nice that you don't really want to do. If a friend is grieving, it takes courage to ask her directly how she is doing.

If we consider only ordinary cases, the nature of courage seems unproblematic. But unusual circumstances present more troublesome cases. Consider the 19 hijackers who murdered almost 3,000 people on September 11, 2001. They faced certain death, evidently without flinching, in the service of an evil cause. Were they courageous? The American political commentator Bill Maher implied that they were, and so his show got canceled. But was he correct? The philosopher Peter Geach (1916–2013) wouldn't think so. "Courage in an unworthy cause," he says, "is no virtue; still less is courage in an evil cause. Indeed I prefer not to call this nonvirtuous facing of danger 'courage.'"

It is easy to see Geach's point. Calling a murderer "courageous" seems to praise his performance, and we don't want to do that. On the other hand, it doesn't seem quite right to say that he is *not* courageous—after all, look at how he behaves in the face of danger. To resolve this dilemma, perhaps we should say that he displays two qualities of character, one admirable (steadfastness in facing danger) and one detestable (a willingness to kill innocent people). He is courageous, as Maher suggested, and courage is a good thing; but because his courage is deployed in such an evil cause, his behavior is *on the whole* extremely wicked.

2. *Generosity.* Generosity is the willingness to give to others. One can be generous with any of one's resources—with one's time, for example, or one's money, or one's knowledge. Aristotle says that generosity, like courage, is a mean between extremes: It falls between stinginess and extravagance. The stingy person gives too little; the extravagant person gives too much; the generous person gives just the right amount. But what amount is just right?

Another ancient teacher, Jesus of Nazareth, said that we must give everything we have to the poor. Jesus considered it wrong to possess riches while other people are starving. Those who heard Jesus speak found his teaching too demanding, and they generally rejected it. Human nature has not changed much in the last 2,000 years: Today, few people follow Jesus's advice, even among those who claim to admire him.

On this issue, the modern utilitarians are Jesus's moral descendants. They hold that in every circumstance it is our duty to do whatever will have the best overall consequences. This means that we should be generous with our money until further giving would harm us as much as it would help others. In other words, we should give until we ourselves become the most worthy recipients of whatever money remains in our hands. If we did this, then we would become poor.

Why do people resist this idea? The main reason may be self-interest; we do not want to become destitute. But this is about more than money; it is also about time and energy. Our lives consist of projects and relationships that require a considerable investment of our money, time, and effort. An ideal of "generosity" that demands too much of us would require us to abandon our normal lives. We'd have to live like saints.

A reasonable interpretation of generosity might, therefore, be something like this: We should be as generous with our resources as we can be while still carrying on our normal lives. Yet even this interpretation leaves us with an awkward question. Some people's "normal lives" are quite extravagant—think of a rich person who has grown accustomed to great luxuries. Surely such a person can't be generous unless he is willing to sell his yacht to feed the hungry. The virtue of generosity, it would seem, cannot exist in the context of a life that is too opulent. So, to make this interpretation of generosity "reasonable," our conception of normal life must not be too extravagant.

3. *Honesty.* The honest person is someone who, first of all, does not lie. But is that enough? Lying is not the only way of misleading people. Geach tells the story of Saint Athanasius, who "was rowing on a river when the persecutors came rowing in the opposite direction: 'Where is the traitor Athanasius?' 'Not far away,' the Saint gaily replied, and rowed past them unsuspected."

Geach approves of the saint's deception, even though he would disapprove of an outright lie. Lying, according to Geach, is always forbidden: someone possessing the virtue of honesty will never even consider it. Honest people do not lie; so, they must find other ways of attaining their goals. Athanasius found such a way, even in his predicament. He did not lie to his pursuers; he "merely" deceived them. But isn't deception dishonest? Why should some ways of misleading people be dishonest, and others not?

To answer that question, let's think about why honesty is a virtue. Why is honesty good? Part of the reason is large-scale: Civilization depends on it. Our ability to live together in communities depends on our ability to communicate. We talk to one another, read each other's writings, exchange information and opinions, express our desires, make promises, ask and answer questions, and much more. Without these sorts of exchanges, social living would be impossible. But people must be honest for such exchanges to work.

On a smaller scale, when we take people at their word, we make ourselves vulnerable to them. By accepting what they say and modifying our behavior accordingly, we place ourselves in their hands. If they speak truthfully, all is well. But if they lie, then we wind up with false beliefs; and if we act on those beliefs, then we do foolish things. We trusted them, and they betrayed our trust. Dishonesty is manipulative. By contrast, honest people treat others with respect.

If these ideas explain why honesty is a virtue, then both lies and "deceptive truths" are dishonest. After all, both are objectionable for the same reasons. Both have the same goal; the point of lying *and* deceiving is to make the listener acquire a false belief. In Geach's example, Athanasius got his persecutors to believe that he was not in fact Athanasius. Had Athanasius lied to his pursuers, rather than merely deceiving them, then his words would have served the same purpose. Because both actions aim at false beliefs, both can disrupt the smooth functioning of society, and both violate trust. If you accuse someone of lying to you, and she responds that she did not lie—she "merely" deceived you—then you would not be impressed. Either way, she took advantage of your trust and manipulated you into believing something false. The honest person will neither lie nor deceive.

But will the honest person *never* lie? Does virtue require adherence to absolute rules? Let's distinguish two positions:

1. An honest person will never lie or deceive.
2. An honest person will never lie or deceive except in rare circumstances when there are compelling reasons to do so.

Despite Geach's protest, there are good reasons to favor the second view, even with regard to lying.

First, remember that honesty is not the only thing we value. In a specific situation, some other value might get priority—for example, the value of self-preservation. Suppose Saint Athanasius had lied and said, "I don't know where that traitor is," and as a result, his pursuers went off on a wild-goose chase. Now the saint would get to live another day. If this had occurred, most of us would continue to regard the saint as honest. We would merely say that he valued his own life more than the telling of one lie.

Moreover, if we consider *why* honesty is good, then we can see that Athanasius would have done nothing wrong by lying to his pursuers. Obviously, that particular lie would not have disrupted the smooth functioning of society. But wouldn't it at least have violated the trust of his pursuers? The response is that, if lying is a violation of trust, then the person you're lying to must *deserve* your trust for the lie to be immoral. Yet in this case, the saint's pursuers did not deserve his trust, because they were persecuting him unjustly. So, even an honest person may sometimes lie or deceive with full justification.

4. *Loyalty to friends and family.* Friendship is essential to the good life. As Aristotle says, "No one would choose to live without friends, even if he had all other goods":

> How could prosperity be safeguarded and preserved without friends? The greater our prosperity is, the greater are the risks it brings with it. Also, in poverty and all other kinds of misfortune, men believe that their only refuge consists in their friends. Friends help young men avoid error; to older people they give the care and help needed to supplement the failing powers of action which infirmity brings.

Of course, the benefits of friendship go far beyond material assistance. Psychologically, we would be lost without our friends. Our triumphs seem hollow without friends to share them with, and we need our friends even more when we fail. Our self-esteem depends largely on their assurances: By returning our affection, our friends confirm our worth as human beings.

If we need friends, then we need the qualities that enable us to *be* a friend. Near the top of the list is loyalty. Friends can be counted on. You stick by your friends even when things are going badly and even when, objectively speaking, you probably should abandon them. Friends make allowances for one another; they forgive offenses and refrain from harsh judgments. There are limits, of course—sometimes only a friend can tell us the hard truth about ourselves. But criticism is acceptable from friends because we know that they are not rejecting us.

The importance of being loyal to friends does not preclude us from having duties to other people, even to strangers. But those duties are associated with different virtues. Generalized beneficence is a virtue, and it may demand a great deal, but it does not require the same level of concern for strangers as for friends. Justice is another such virtue; it requires impartial treatment for all. But the demands of justice are weaker when friends are involved, because loyalty requires at least somewhat partial treatment.

We are even closer to family members than we are to friends, so we may show family members even more loyalty and partiality. In Plato's *Euthyphro*, Socrates learns that Euthyphro has come to the courthouse to testify against his own father, who is on trial for murder. Socrates expresses surprise at this and wonders whether a son should bear witness against his father. Euthyphro sees no impropriety: For him, a murder is a murder. Euthyphro has a point, but we might still be shocked that someone could take the same attitude toward his father that he would take toward a stranger. A close family member, we might think, need not be involved in such a case. This point is recognized in American law: In the United States, one cannot be compelled to testify in court against one's husband or wife.

Why Are the Virtues Important? We said that virtues are traits of character that are good for people to have. This raises the question of why the virtues are good. Why should a person be courageous, generous, honest, or loyal? The answer may depend on the virtue in question. Thus:

- Courage is good because we need it to cope with danger.
- Generosity is desirable because there will always be people who need help.

- Honesty is needed because without it relations between people would go wrong in all sorts of ways.
- Loyalty is essential to friendship; friends stand by one another even when others would turn away.

This list suggests that each virtue is valuable for a different reason. However, Aristotle offers a general answer to our question—he says that the virtues are important because the virtuous person will fare better in life. The point is not that the virtuous will always be richer; the point is that the virtuous will flourish.

To see what Aristotle means, consider some basic facts about human nature. On the most general level, human beings are social creatures who want the company of others. So we live in communities among family, friends, and fellow citizens. In this setting, such qualities as loyalty, fairness, and honesty are needed to interact successfully with others. On a more individual level, a person might have a particular job and pursue particular interests. Those endeavors might call for other virtues, such as diligence and conscientiousness. Finally, it is part of our common human condition that we must sometimes face danger or temptation, so courage and self-control are needed. Thus, the virtues all have the same general sort of value: they are all qualities needed for successful living.

Are the Virtues the Same for Everyone? Finally, we may ask whether a single set of traits is desirable for all people. Should we speak of *the* good person, as though all good people were alike? Friedrich Nietzsche (1844–1900) thought not. In his flamboyant way, Nietzsche observes,

> How naive it is altogether to say: "Man *ought* to be such-and-such!" Reality shows us an enchanting wealth of types, the abundance of a lavish play and change of forms—and some wretched loafer of a moralist comments: "No! Man ought to be different." He even knows what man should be like, this wretched bigot and prig: he paints himself on the wall and comments, *"Ecce homo!"* ["Behold the man!"]

There is obviously something to this. The scholar who devotes his life to understanding medieval literature and the professional soldier are very different kinds of people. A Victorian woman who would never expose a leg in public and a woman who sunbathes on a nude beach may have very different lifestyles. And yet each may be admirable.

There is, then, an obvious sense in which the virtues may differ from person to person. Because people lead different kinds of lives, have different sorts of personalities, and occupy different social roles, the qualities of character that help them flourish may differ.

It is tempting to go even further and say that the virtues differ from society to society. After all, the kind of life that is possible will depend on the values and institutions that dominate a region. A scholar's life is possible only where there are institutions, such as universities, that make intellectual investigation possible. Much the same could be said about being an athlete, a geisha, a social worker, or a samurai warrior. Different character traits are needed to occupy each role successfully. Thus, the virtues will be different.

To this, it may be answered that *certain virtues will be needed by all people in all times*. This was Aristotle's view, and he was probably right. Aristotle believed that we all have a great deal in common, despite our differences. "One may observe," he says, "in one's travels to distant countries the feelings of recognition and affiliation that link every human being to every other human being." Even in the most disparate societies, people face the same basic problems and have the same basic needs. Thus:

- Everyone needs courage, because no one (not even the scholar) can always avoid danger. Also, everyone needs the courage to take the occasional risk.
- In every society, there will be some people who are worse off than others; so, generosity will always be prized.
- Honesty is always a virtue because no society can exist without dependable communication.
- Everyone needs friends, and to have friends one must be a friend; so, everyone needs loyalty.

The major virtues flow from our common human condition; they are not determined by social custom.

12.3. Two Advantages of Virtue Ethics

Virtue Ethics is often said to have two selling points.

1. *Moral motivation.* Virtue Ethics is appealing because it provides a natural and attractive account of moral motivation. Consider the following:

You are in the hospital recovering from a long illness. You are bored and restless, and so you are delighted when Smith comes to visit. You have a good time talking to him; his visit really cheers you up. After a while, you tell Smith how much you enjoy seeing him—he really is a good friend to take the trouble to come see you. But, Smith says, he is merely doing his duty. At first you think he is only being modest, but the more you talk, the clearer it becomes that he is speaking the literal truth. He is not visiting you because he wants to or because he likes you, but only because he thinks he should "do the right thing." He feels it is his duty to visit you, perhaps because you are worse off than anyone else he knows.

This example was suggested by the American philosopher Michael Stocker (1940–). As Stocker points out, you'd be very disappointed to learn Smith's motive; now his visit seems cold and calculated. You thought he was your friend, but now you know otherwise. Commenting on Smith's behavior, Stocker says, "Surely there is something lacking here—and lacking in moral merit or value."

Of course, there is nothing wrong with *what* Smith did. The problem is *why* he did it. We value friendship, love, and respect, and we want our relationships to be based on mutual regard. Acting from an abstract sense of duty or from a desire to "do the right thing" is not the same. We would not want to live among people who acted only from such motives, nor would we want to be such a person ourselves. Therefore, the argument goes, theories that focus on right action cannot provide a full account of the moral life. For that, we need a theory that emphasizes personal qualities such as friendship, love, and loyalty—in other words, a theory of the virtues.

2. *Doubts about the "ideal" of impartiality.* A dominant theme in modern moral philosophy has been impartiality—the idea that all persons are morally equal, and that we should treat everyone's interests as equally important. The utilitarian theory is typical. "Utilitarianism," John Stuart Mill writes, "requires [the moral agent] to be as strictly impartial as a disinterested and benevolent spectator." The book you are now reading also treats impartiality as fundamental to ethics: In the first chapter, impartiality was included in the "minimum conception" of morality.

It may be doubted, though, whether impartiality is really such a noble ideal. Consider our relationships with family and friends. Should we be impartial where their interests are concerned? A mother loves her children and cares for them in a way that she does not care for other children. She is partial to them, through and through. Is anything wrong with that? Isn't that exactly the way a mother should be? Again, we love our friends, and we are willing to do things for them that we would not do for others. What's wrong with that? Loving relationships are essential to the good life. But any theory that emphasizes impartiality will have a hard time accounting for this.

A moral theory that emphasizes the virtues, however, can easily account for all this. Some virtues are partial and some are not. Loyalty involves partiality toward loved ones and friends; beneficence involves equal regard for everyone. What is needed is not some general requirement of impartiality, but an understanding of how these virtues relate to one another.

12.4. Virtue and Conduct

As we have seen, theories that emphasize right action seem incomplete because they neglect the question of character. Virtue Ethics remedies this problem by making character its central concern. But as a result, Virtue Ethics runs the risk of being incomplete in the other direction. Moral problems are frequently problems about what to *do*. What can a theory of virtue tell us about the assessment, not of character, but of action?

The answer will depend on the spirit with which Virtue Ethics is offered. On the one hand, we might combine the best features of the right-action approach with insights drawn from the virtues approach. For example, we might try to improve Utilitarianism or Kantianism by supplementing them with a theory of moral character. This seems sensible. If so, then we can assess right action simply by relying on Utilitarianism or Kantianism.

On the other hand, some writers believe that Virtue Ethics should be understood as an *alternative* to the other theories. They believe that Virtue Ethics is a complete moral theory in itself. We might call this *Radical Virtue Ethics*. What would such a theory say about right action? Either it will need to dispense with the notion of "right action" altogether, or it will need to derive an account of it from the conception of virtuous character.

It might sound extreme, but some philosophers have taken the first approach, arguing that we should get rid of such concepts as "morally right action." Anscombe would consider it "a great improvement" if we stopped using such notions. We could still assess conduct as better or worse, she says, but we would do so in other terms. Instead of calling an action "morally wrong," we would call it "intolerant" or "unjust" or "cowardly"–terms taken from the vocabulary of virtue. On her view, such terms allow us to say everything that needs to be said.

But advocates of Radical Virtue Ethics need not reject notions such as "morally right." These ideas can be retained but given a new interpretation within the virtue framework. We could still assess actions based on the reasons that can be given for or against them. However, *the reasons cited will always be connected with the virtues.* Thus, the reasons for doing some particular action might be that it is honest, or generous, or fair; while the reasons against doing it might be that it is dishonest, or stingy, or unfair. On this approach, the right thing to do is whatever a virtuous person would do.

12.5. The Problem of Incompleteness

The main objection to Radical Virtue Ethics is that it is incomplete. It seems to be incomplete in three ways.

First, Radical Virtue Ethics cannot explain everything it should explain. Consider a typical virtue, such as dependability. Why should I be dependable? Plainly, we need an answer that goes beyond the simple observation that dependability is a virtue. We want to know *why* it is a virtue; we want to know why it is good. Possible explanations might be that being dependable is to one's own advantage, or that being dependable promotes the general welfare, or that dependability is needed by those who must live together and rely on one another. The first explanation looks suspiciously like Ethical

Egoism; the second is utilitarian; and the third recalls the Social Contract Theory. But none of these explanations are couched in terms of the virtues. Any explanation of why a particular virtue is good, it seems, would have to take us beyond the narrow confines of Radical Virtue Ethics.

If Radical Virtue Ethics doesn't explain *why* something is a virtue, then it won't be able to tell us whether the virtues apply in difficult cases. Consider the virtue of being beneficent, or being kind. Suppose I hear some news that would upset you to know about. Maybe I've learned that someone you used to know died in a car accident. If I don't tell you this, you might never find out. Suppose, also, that you're the sort of person who would want to be told. If I know all this, should I tell you the news? What would be the *kind* thing to do? It's a hard question, because what you would prefer—being told—conflicts with what would make you feel good— not being told. Would a kind person care more about what you want or more about what makes you feel good? Radical Virtue Ethics cannot answer this question. To be kind is to look out for someone's best interests; but Radical Virtue Ethics does not tell us what someone's best interests are. So, the second way in which the theory is incomplete is that it cannot give us a full interpretation of the virtues. In particular, it cannot say exactly when they apply.

Finally, Radical Virtue Ethics is incomplete because it cannot help us deal with cases of moral conflict. Suppose I just got a haircut—a mullet the likes of which have not been seen in some time—and I put you on the spot by asking you what you think. You can either tell me the truth, or you can say that I look just fine. Honesty and kindness are both virtues, and so there are reasons both for and against each alternative. But you must do one or the other— you must either tell the truth and be unkind, or tell a lie and be kind. Which should you do? If someone told you, "You should act virtuously in this situation," that wouldn't help you decide what to do; it would only leave you wondering which virtue to abide by. Clearly, we need guidance beyond the resources of Radical Virtue Ethics.

By itself, Radical Virtue Ethics seems to be limited to platitudes: be kind, be honest, be patient, be generous, and so on. Platitudes are vague, and when they conflict, we must look beyond them for guidance. Radical Virtue Ethics needs the resources of a larger theory.

12.6. Conclusion

It seems best to regard Virtue Ethics as part of our overall theory of ethics rather than as being complete in itself. The total theory would include an account of all the considerations that figure in practical decision-making, together with their underlying rationales. The question is whether such a theory can accommodate both an adequate conception of right action and a related conception of virtuous character.

I don't see why not. Suppose, for example, that we accept a utilitarian theory of right action—we believe that one ought to do whatever will lead to the most happiness. From a moral point of view, we would want a society in which everyone leads happy and satisfying lives. We could then ask which actions, which social policies, *and which qualities of character* would be most likely to produce that result. An inquiry into the nature of virtue could then be conducted from within that larger framework.

Notes on Sources

Aristotle is quoted from book 2 of the *Nicomachean Ethics*, translated by Martin Ostwald (Indianapolis: Bobbs-Merrill, 1962), except for the passage about friendship (from book 8) and the passage about visiting foreign lands, which is Martha C. Nussbaum's translation in "Non-Relative Virtues: An Aristotelian Approach," *Midwest Studies in Philosophy*, vol. 13: *Ethical Theory: Character and Virtue*, edited by Peter A. French et al. (University of Notre Dame Press, 1988), pp. 32-53.

Pincoffs's suggestion about the nature of virtue appears in his book *Quandaries and Virtues: Against Reductivism in Ethics* (Lawrence: University of Kansas Press, 1986), p. 78.

Peter Geach, *The Virtues* (Cambridge: Cambridge University Press, 1977). On courage: p. xxx; on Saint Athanasius: p. 114.

Jesus says that we should give all we have to help the poor in Matthew 19:21-24, Mark 10:21-25, and Luke 18:22-25.

Plato's *Euthyphro* has several translations, including Hugh Tredennick and Harold Tarrant's in *Plato: The Last Days of Socrates* (New York: Penguin Books, 2003), pp. 19-41.

Nietzsche is quoted from his *Twilight of the Idols*, "Morality as Anti-Nature," pt. 6, translated by Walter Kaufmann in *The Portable Nietzsche* (New York: Viking Press, 1954), p. 491.

Michael Stocker, "The Schizophrenia of Modern Ethical Theories," *Journal of Philosophy* 73 (1976), pp. 453-466.

John Stuart Mill is quoted from *Utilitarianism*, chapter 2 (1861). Elizabeth Anscombe rejects the notion of "morally right" in "Modern Moral Philosophy," *Philosophy* 33 (1958), pp. 1–19, reprinted in *Ethics, Religion and Politics: The Collected Philosophical Papers of G. E. M. Anscombe*, vol. 3 (University of Minnesota Press, 1981), pp. 26–42 ("it would be a great improvement": p. 33).

CHAPTER 13

*W*hat Would a Satisfactory Moral Theory Be Like?

Some people believe that there cannot be progress in Ethics, since everything has already been said. . . . I believe the opposite. . . . Compared with the other sciences, Non-Religious Ethics is the youngest and least advanced.

DEREK PARFIT, *REASONS AND PERSONS* (1984)

13.1. Morality without Hubris

Moral philosophy has a rich and fascinating history. Scholars have approached the subject from many different perspectives, producing theories that both attract and repel the thoughtful reader. All of the classical theories contain plausible elements, which is hardly surprising, because they were devised by philosophers of undoubted genius. Yet the various theories conflict with each other, and most of them seem vulnerable to crippling objections. Thus, one is left wondering what to believe. What, in the final analysis, is the truth?

Naturally, different philosophers would answer this question in different ways. Some might refuse to give an answer, on the grounds that we do not know enough to offer a "final analysis." In this respect, moral philosophy is not much worse off than any other subject—we do not know the final truth about most things. But we do know a lot, and it might not be rash to say something about what a satisfactory moral theory might be like.

A Modest Conception of Human Beings. A satisfactory theory would be realistic about where human beings fit in the grand

186

scheme of things. The "big bang" occurred some 13.8 billion years ago, and the earth was formed around 4.5 billion years ago. Life on earth evolved slowly, mostly according to the principles of natural selection. When the dinosaurs went extinct 65 million years ago, this left more room for the evolution of mammals, and a few hundred thousand years ago, one line of that evolution produced us. In geological time, we arrived only yesterday.

But no sooner did our ancestors arrive than they began to think of themselves as the crown of creation. Some of them even imagined that the whole universe had been made for their benefit. Thus, when they began to develop theories of right and wrong, they held that their own interests had a kind of ultimate and objective value. The rest of creation, they reasoned, was intended for their use. But now we know better. We now know that we exist by evolutionary accident, as one species among millions, on one small speck of an unimaginably vast cosmos. The details of this picture are revised each year, as more is discovered, but the main outlines are well established. Some of the old story remains: human beings are still the smartest animals we know and the only ones that use language. Those facts, however, cannot justify an entire worldview that places us at the center.

How Reason Gives Rise to Ethics. Human beings have evolved as rational beings. Because we are rational, we are able to take some facts as reasons for behaving one way rather than another. We can articulate those reasons and think about them. Thus, if an action would help to satisfy our desires, needs, and so on—in short, if it would *promote our interests*—then we take that as a reason to do it.

The origin of our concept of "ought" may be found in these facts. If we were incapable of considering reasons, we would have no use for such a notion. Like the other animals, we would act from instinct, habit, or passing desire. But the examination of reasons introduces a new factor. Now we find ourselves driven to act in certain ways as a result of deliberation—as a result of thinking about our behavior and its consequences. We use the word "ought" to mark this new element of the situation: We ought to do what there are the strongest reasons for doing.

Once we see morality as a matter of acting on reason, another important point emerges. In reasoning about what to do, we can be consistent or inconsistent. One way of being inconsistent is to accept a fact as a reason on one occasion but to reject it as a reason on a similar occasion. This happens when one places the interests of one's own race above the interests of other races, despite the similarity of the races. Racism is an offense against morality because it is an offense against reason. Similar remarks apply to other doctrines that divide humanity into the morally favored and disfavored, such as nationalism, sexism, and classism. The upshot is that reason requires impartiality: We ought to promote the interests of everyone alike.

If Psychological Egoism were true—if we could care only about ourselves—this would mean that reason demands more of us than we can manage. But Psychological Egoism is not true; it presents a false picture of human nature and the human condition. We have evolved as social creatures, living together in groups, wanting one another's company, needing one another's cooperation, and caring about one another's welfare. So there is a pleasing "fit" between (a) what reason requires, namely, impartiality; (b) the requirements of social living, namely, adherence to rules that serve everyone's interests, if fairly applied; and (c) our natural inclination to care about others—although, admittedly, we should care about others even more than we naturally do. Thus, morality is not only *possible* for us; to a large extent, it is natural for us.

13.2. Treating People as They Deserve

The idea that we should "promote the interests of everyone alike" is appealing when it is used to refute bigotry. However, sometimes there is good reason to treat people differently—sometimes people *deserve* to be treated better or worse than others. Human beings are rational agents who can make free choices. Those who choose to treat others well deserve good treatment; those who choose to treat others badly deserve ill treatment.

This sounds harsh until we consider some examples. Suppose Smith has always been generous, helping you whenever she could, and now she is in trouble and needs your help. You now have a special reason to help her, beyond the general obligation you have to be helpful to everyone. She is not just a member of the great crowd of humanity; she has earned your respect and gratitude through her conduct.

By contrast, consider someone with the opposite history. Your neighbor Jones has always refused to be helpful. One day, for example, your car wouldn't start, and he wouldn't give you a ride to work—he just couldn't be bothered. Some time later, though, *he* has car trouble and asks *you* for a ride. Now Jones deserves to have to fend for himself. If you gave him a ride despite his past behavior, you would be choosing to treat him better than he deserves.

Treating people as they have chosen to treat others is not just a matter of rewarding friends and holding grudges against enemies. It is a matter of treating people as responsible agents who merit particular responses, based on their past conduct. There is an important difference between Smith and Jones: One of them deserves our gratitude; the other deserves our resentment. What would it be like if we did not care about such things?

For one thing, we would be denying people the ability to earn good treatment at the hands of others. This is important. Because we live in communities, how each of us fares depends not only on what we do but on what others do as well. If we are to flourish, then we need others to treat us well. A social system in which deserts are acknowledged gives us a way of doing that; it gives us the power to determine our own fates.

Absent this, what could we do? We might imagine a system in which a person can get good treatment only by force, or by luck, or as a matter of charity. But the practice of acknowledging deserts is different. It not only gives people an incentive to treat others well but also gives them control over how they themselves will be treated. It says to them, "If you behave well, you will be *entitled* to good treatment from others. You will have earned it." Acknowledging deserts is ultimately about treating other people with respect.

13.3. A Variety of Motives

There are other ways in which the idea of "promoting the interests of everyone alike" apparently fails to capture the whole of moral life. (I say "apparently" because I will ask later whether it really does.)

Certainly, people should sometimes be moved by an impartial concern for others. But there are other morally praiseworthy motives:

- A mother loves and cares for her children. She does not want to "promote their interests" simply because they are people she can help. Her attitude toward them is entirely different from her attitude toward other children.
- A man is loyal to his friends. Again, he is not concerned with their interests only as part of his general concern for people. They are his friends, and so they matter more to him.

Only a philosophical fool would want to eliminate love, loyalty, and the like from our understanding of the moral life. If such motives were eliminated, and instead people simply calculated what was best, we would all be much worse off. Anyway, who would want to live in a world without love and friendship?

Of course, people may have other good motives:

- A composer is concerned, above all else, to finish her symphony. She pursues this even though she might do "more good" by doing something else.
- A teacher devotes great effort to preparing his classes, even though he might do more good by directing his energy elsewhere.

While these motives are not usually considered "moral," we should not want to eliminate them from human life. Taking pride in one's job, wanting to create something of value, and many other noble intentions contribute to both personal happiness and the general welfare. We should no more want to eliminate them than to eliminate love and friendship.

13.4. Multiple-Strategies Utilitarianism

Above, I tried to justify the principle that "we ought to act so as to promote the interests of everyone alike." But then I noted that this cannot be the whole story of our moral obligations because, sometimes, we should treat different people differently, according to their individual deserts. And then I discussed some morally important motives that seem unrelated to the impartial promotion of interests.

Yet these concerns may be interrelated. At first blush, it seems that treating people according to their individual deserts is quite different from seeking to promote the interests of everyone alike. But when we asked why deserts are important, the answer was that *we would all be much worse off* if acknowledging deserts was not part of our social scheme. And when we ask why love, friendship, artistic creativity, and pride in one's work are important, the answer is that *our lives would be so much poorer* without them. This suggests that a single standard might be at work in our assessments.

Perhaps, then, the single moral standard is human welfare. What is important is that people be as happy as possible. This standard can be used to assess a wide variety of things, including actions, policies, social customs, laws, rules, motives, and character traits. But this does not mean that we should always think in terms of making people as happy as possible. Our day-to-day lives will go better if we simply love our children, enjoy our friends, take pride in our work, keep our promises, and so on. An ethic that values "the interests of everyone alike" will endorse this conclusion.

This is an old idea. The great utilitarian theorist Henry Sidgwick (1838–1900) made the same point:

> The doctrine that Universal Happiness is the ultimate *standard* must not be understood to imply that Universal Benevolence is the only right or always best *motive* of action . . . if experience shows that the general happiness will be more satisfactorily attained if men frequently act from other motives than pure universal philanthropy, it is obvious that these other motives are reasonably to be preferred on Utilitarian principles.

This passage has been cited in support of a view called "Motive Utilitarianism." According to that view, we should act from the motives that best promote the general welfare.

Yet the most plausible view of this type does not focus exclusively on motives; nor does it focus entirely on acts or rules, as other theories have done. The most plausible theory might be called *Multiple-Strategies Utilitarianism*. This theory is utilitarian, because the ultimate goal is to maximize the general welfare. However, it recognizes that we may use diverse strategies to pursue that goal. Sometimes we may aim directly at it. For example, a senator may support a bill because she believes that it would raise the standard of living for everyone. Or an individual may send money to the International Red Cross because he believes that this would do more good than anything else he could do. But usually we don't (and needn't) think of the general welfare at all; instead, we simply care for our children, work at our jobs, obey the law, keep our promises, and so on.

Right Action as Living According to the Best Plan. We can make the idea behind Multiple-Strategies Utilitarianism a little more specific.

Suppose we had a fully specified list of the virtues, motives, and methods of decision-making that would enable a person to be happy and to contribute to the welfare of others. And suppose, further, that this list is *optimal* for that person; no other combination of features would work better. Such a list would include at least the following:

- The virtues that are needed to make one's life go well
- The motives on which to act
- The commitments that one will have to friends, family, and others
- The social roles that one will occupy, with the responsibilities and demands that go with them
- The duties and concerns associated with one's projects and one's choice of career
- The everyday rules that one will usually follow without even thinking
- A strategy, or group of strategies, about when to consider making exceptions to the rules, and the grounds on which those exceptions can be made

The list would also specify the relations between the different items on the list—what takes priority over what, how to adjudicate conflicts, and so on. It would be very hard to construct such a list. As a practical matter, it might even be impossible. But we can be fairly sure that it would include endorsements of friendship, honesty, and other familiar virtues. It would tell us to keep our promises, but not always, and to refrain from harming people, but not always, and so on. And it would probably tell us to stop living in luxury while millions of children die of preventable diseases.

At any rate, there is some combination of virtues, motives, and methods of decision-making that is best *for me*, given my circumstances, personality, and talents—"best" in the sense that it will optimize my chances of having a good life, while optimizing the chances of other people having good lives, too. Call this optimum combination *my best plan*. The right thing for me to do is to act in accordance with my best plan.

My best plan may have a lot in common with yours. Presumably, they will both include rules against lying, stealing, and killing, together with an understanding about when to make exceptions to those rules. They will each include virtues such as patience, kindness, and self-control. They may both contain instructions for raising children, including a specification of the virtues to foster in them.

But our best plans need not be identical. People have different personalities and talents. One person may find fulfillment as a rabbi while someone else could never live like that. Thus, our lives might include different sorts of personal relationships, and we might need to cultivate different virtues. People also live in different circumstances and have access to different resources—some are rich; some are poor; some are privileged; some are persecuted. Thus, the optimum strategies for living will differ.

In each case, however, the identification of a plan as the best plan will be a matter of assessing how well it promotes the interests of everyone alike. So the overall theory is utilitarian, even though it may frequently endorse motives that do not sound utilitarian at all.

13.5. The Moral Community

As moral agents, we should be concerned with everyone whose welfare we might affect. This may seem like a pious platitude, but in reality it can be a hard doctrine. Around the world, many children fail to get essential vaccinations, resulting in hundreds of thousands of unnecessary deaths each year. Citizens in the richer countries could easily cut these numbers in half, but they don't. People would no doubt do more if children in their own neighborhoods were dying, but the children's location shouldn't matter: Everyone is included in the community of moral concern. If we cared about all children, then we'd have to change our ways.

Just as the moral community is not limited to people in one *place*, so it is not limited to people at any one *time*. Whether people will be affected by our actions now or in the future is irrelevant. Our obligation is to consider everyone's interests equally. One consequence of this pertains to nuclear weapons. Such weapons not only have the power to maim and kill innocent people, but they can also poison the environment for thousands of years. If the welfare of future generations is given proper weight, it is difficult to imagine any circumstance in which such weapons should be used. Climate change is another issue that affects the interests of our descendants. If we fail to reverse the effects of global warming, our children will suffer even more than we will.

There is one other way in which our conception of the moral community must be expanded. Humans are not alone on this planet. Other sentient animals—that is, animals capable of feeling pleasure and pain—also have interests. When we abuse or kill them, they are harmed, just as such actions can harm humans. We must, therefore, include the interests of nonhuman animals in our calculations. As Jeremy Bentham (1748–1832) pointed out, excluding creatures from moral consideration because of their species is no more justified than excluding them because of their race, nationality, or income level. The single moral standard is not human welfare, but all welfare.

13.6. Justice and Fairness

Utilitarianism has been criticized as unfair and unjust. Can the complications we have introduced help?

One criticism concerns punishment. We can imagine cases in which it would promote the general welfare to frame an innocent person. Such an act would be blatantly unjust, yet Utilitarianism seems to require it. More generally, as Kant pointed out, utilitarians are happy to "use" criminals to achieve the goals of society. Even if those goals are worthwhile—such as the reduction of crime—we might be uncomfortable with a theory that endorses manipulation as a legitimate moral strategy.

However, our theory takes a different view of punishment than most utilitarians have taken. In fact, our view is closer to Kant's.

In punishing someone, we are treating him worse than we treat others. But this is justified by the person's own past deeds: It is a response to what he has done. That is why it is not right to frame an innocent person; the innocent person has done nothing to deserve such treatment.

The theory of punishment, however, is only one aspect of justice. Questions of justice arise whenever someone is treated better or worse than someone else. Suppose an employer must choose which of two employees to promote. The first candidate has worked hard, taking on extra work, giving up vacation time, and so on. The second candidate, on the other hand, has never done more than he had to. Obviously, the two employees will be treated very differently: One will get promoted; one will not. But this is all right, according to our theory. The first employee has earned the promotion; the second has not.

Often, people think it is right for individuals to be rewarded for physical beauty, superior intelligence, and other qualities that are due, in large part, to having the right DNA and being raised by the right parents. The real world reflects this: Individuals often have better jobs and more money just because they were born with greater natural gifts or into a wealthier family. But, on reflection, this does not seem right. People do not deserve their native endowments; they have them only as a result of what John Rawls (1921–2002) calls "the natural lottery." Suppose the first employee in our example was passed over for the promotion, despite her hard work, because the second employee had some natural ability that was more useful in the new position. Even if the employer could justify this decision in terms of the company's needs, the first employee would rightly feel cheated. She has worked harder, yet he is getting the promotion and the benefits that go with it because of something he did nothing to earn. That is not fair. In a just society, people could improve their circumstances through hard work, but they would not benefit from a lucky birth.

13.7. Conclusion

What would a satisfactory moral theory look like? I have outlined the possibility that seems most plausible to me: According to Multiple-Strategies Utilitarianism, we should maximize the interests of all sentient beings by living according to our best plan. One must be modest, however, in making such a proposal. Over the centuries, ethicists have articulated and defended a wide variety of theories, and history has always found flaws in their conceptions. Still, there is hope, if not for my suggestion, then for some other proposal down the road. Civilization is only a few thousand years old. If we do not destroy it, then the study of moral philosophy has a bright future.

Notes on Sources

The age of the universe was estimated by scientists from data gathered by the European Space Agency's "Planck" observatory from 2009 to 2013.

    Henry Sidgwick, *The Methods of Ethics*, 7th ed. (London: Macmillan, 1907), p. 413.

    John Rawls discusses the "natural lottery" in *A Theory of Justice* (Cambridge, MA: Harvard University Press, 1971), p. 74 (and on p. 64 of the revised edition from 1999).

Index

197